BARNGA

BARNGA

A SIMULATION GAME ON CULTURAL CLASHES

25th Anniversary Edition
Revised and Enhanced

Sivasailam "Thiagi" Thiagarajan

with Raja Thiagarajan

INTERCULTURAL PRESS
A Nicholas Brealey Publishing Company

BOSTON • LONDON

First published by Intercultural Press,
a Nicholas Brealey Publishing Company, in 2006.

Intercultural Press, a division
of Nicholas Brealey Publishing
100 City Hall Plaza, Suite 501
Boston, MA 02108 USA
Tel: (+) 617-523-3801
Fax: (+) 617-523-3708
www.interculturalpress.com

Nicholas Brealey Publishing
3-5 Spafield Street, Clerkenwell
London, EC1R 4QB, UK
Tel: +44-(0)-207-239-0360
Fax: +44-(0)-207-239-0370
www.nbrealey-books.com

© 2006 by Sivasailam Thiagarajan

10 09 08 07 06   1 2 3 4 5

ISBN-13: 978-1-931930-30-7
ISBN-10: 1-931930-30-9

Library of Congress Cataloging-in-Publication Data
Thiagarajan, Sivasailam.
Barnga : a simulation game on cultural clashes / Sivasailam "Thiagi"
Thiagarajan with Raja Thiagarajan.—25th anniversary ed.,
Rev. and enhanced.
        p.   cm.
ISBN-13: 978-1-931930-30-7
ISBN-10: 1-931930-30-9
1. Intercultural communication—Study and teaching—Simulation methods.
I. Thiagarajan, Raja.   II. Title.
GN345.6.T48 2006
303.48'2071—dc22   2006002324

Acknowledgments

I want to thank several people who made BARNGA possible:

- the late Barbara Steinwachs for her enthusiastic dedication to this simulation game and to the use of simulation gaming in general.
- people associated with the earlier version of BARNGA, especially Pierre Corbeil and Peggy Pusch.
- people associated with this version of BARNGA, especially to my publisher Patricia O'Hare, my dedicated proofreader Jean Reese, and my translators Nancy Bragard, Samuel van den Bergh, Ivan Cortes, and Alexandra Cortes.
- my friends from the Society for Intercultural Education, Training and Research (SIETAR), especially Judee Blohm, Sandy Fowler, and Heather Robinson.
- hundreds of facilitators around the world who conducted BARNGA during the past two decades.
- my Liberian friends and the International members of the project team who worked and played with me in Gbarnga.
- my family: Lucy, Raja, Julie, Jason, Matt, Kat, and Lia.

To the memory of
Aida L. Pasigna
My friend and colleague in Gbarnga and in Bloomington

Contents

- **French**

  Transparency Masters

  CINQ PLIS

  CINQ PLIS pour Trois Joueurs

- **German**

  Transparency Masters

  FÜNF STICHE

  FÜNF STICHE für Drei Spieler

- **Spanish**

  Transparency Masters

  CINCO TRUCOS

  CINCO TRUCOS para Tres Jugadores

How It All Started

The loud banging on the door woke me up at 3:30 in the morning. I staggered to the front of the house, undid the four bolts, and opened the heavy door to confront three armed rebels, two in camouflage fatigues and one wearing a Michael Jordan T-shirt.

The man in the T-shirt said hoarsely, "Give us the keys to your vehicles."

He reeked of beer and stumbled over the word "vehicles."

Feigning innocence, I asked him, "Who are you and do you have some authorization?"

The man pointed his rifle to my head. One of the other soldiers did the same.

"This is all the authority we need, old man. We are now the government. The vehicles belong to us. So give us keys quick."

I silently handed him the keys to the five trucks.

That was the morning of Sunday, April 13, 1980. I was the Chief of Party for a USAID-sponsored primary education project in Liberia. I lived in a large house in a small town called Gbarnga with my wife Lucy and my son Raja. My exalted title and the large house resulted in all the project trucks being parked in front of my house at night. During the day, the trucks transported instructional materials to 30 primary schools in 12 different Liberian counties.

On the day before, we took one of the trucks for a ride to the market in Ganta in the nearby Nimba County. Around noon, on our way back, we stopped at a roadside gas pump in Palala. Mamadi, our driver, got into a conversation with the person who hand-pumped the gas. When he came back, Mamadi reported that there was a coup in Monrovia, the capital city, and the army had taken over the country. We thought it was just an exaggerated rumor until we got back home and listened to BBC. Master Sergeant Samuel K. Doe had indeed taken over the government.

We decided to stay home, but Lucy insisted on visiting Aida and Becky, two Philippina members of the project team who lived about a mile away. They both declined our invitation to stay with us, feeling safe because they felt that their neighbors would protect them. Later that evening we heard sporadic gunfire near the Gbarnga market but we were told that it was just the citizen-soldiers celebrating their freedom.

Without our vehicles, we stayed home the next week. We closed down the project office to prevent looting. Many of our Liberian colleagues visited us frequently and gave us the latest news about which cabinet members had been decapitated. We spent most evenings playing Scrabble with Samba, Edwin, and Elizabeth.

For a change of pace—and also for providing equal opportunity—to my Liberian colleagues who had not memorized esoteric two- and three-letter words, I decided to take up playing card games. I chose EUCHRE, a popular Hoosier game. I lent my *Hoyle's* to potential players to read and master the rules of the game.

That was an interesting experiment. Tuesday, we started playing the game after everyone assured me that they knew the rules. After about 5 minutes, it became very clear that each person had a different interpretation of the same rules. This resulted in some quarrels about trumps, accusations about cheating, and complaints about lack of intelligence. The most interesting thing was that everyone was sure that his interpretation of the rules was the correct one. In the heat of the argument, my friends appealed to me for mediation and resolution. Out of sheer mischief, I feigned ignorance of the official rules and proclaimed that I was willing to abide by whatever they all agreed to be the standard set of rules. It took my friends a 3-hour palaver before they concurred on the rules they wanted to play by. These rules were not the same that my friends in Bloomington played by, but they seemed to work

This interesting episode presented me with a blinding flash of the obvious:

Serious conflicts arise not from major, obvious cultural differences, but from unrecognized, minor ones.

During the EUCHRE episode, I was intrigued by the misinterpretation of the rules and the comical consequences that arose when everyone assumed that they were playing by the same set of rules. All the arguments, misunderstandings, accusations, negotiations, and emotional attachment to one's own set of rules reflected what happens when people from different cultures interact with each other.

What would happen, I thought, if we deliberately give different rules to different people and pretended that everyone is playing by the same rules?

This was the orgin of BARNGA, the simulation game—and its name.

I wrote up the directions for playing BARNGA during the week immediately after the coup. We all stayed in Gbarnga and I continued to direct the project for the next 18 months. After my return to the United States, I facilitated BARNGA with a several groups of participants interested in diversity and intercultural communication. I also shared the manual with my friends and since I believe that the simulation game always belongs to the facilitator, I encouraged them to experiment with modifications. The late Barbara Steinwachs (my friend from the North American Simulation and Gaming Association [NASAGA] and the Society for Intercultural Education, Training and Research [SIETAR]) gave BARNGA a boost by getting the manual published by Intercultural Press. I am extremely grateful to the publisher and I was surprised when BARNGA became a popular cult item and I was irritated because it sold more copies than many of the better simulation games that I had designed. I started receiving thank-you notes from facilitators and players in Tokyo, Jakarta, Zurich, Melbourne, Moscow, Hong Kong, and other such faraway places. For various reasons, this simulation game appears to strike a universal chord among diverse cultures around the world.

More than 25 years since I first played BARNGA in Gbarnga, I have rewritten the manual, retaining the original flow and incorporating some recent embellishments.

What's BARNGA All About?

Before getting into the step-by-step details of the simulation game, let's take a quick look at the big picture.

Purpose

BARNGA is designed to explore factors related to communication problems in intercultural situations. The term *culture* is used broadly; for example, the game could be used to explore communication problems among people in different departments. Specifically, BARNGA entraps participants into assuming that everyone abides by the same rules of acceptable behavior. BARNGA points out that obvious cultural differences create fewer problems than subtle differences.

Participants

You need at least eight players to play BARNGA. (If you have fewer players, see the chapter How to Modify BARNGA.) The best game involves 20 to 40 players.

Time Requirements

The actual play of the game takes about 20 to 30 minutes. You should set aside an equal amount of time for debriefing.

Supplies

- 1 deck of playing cards for each group of four players
- 1 set of handouts for each group of four players

Flow of the Game

Organize groups. Divide participants into groups of four. (If there are any leftover participants, they can assist you.) Seat each group of four at a table.

Distribute handouts. Give each group a set of handouts that explains how to play a card game called FIVE TRICKS. Participants will think they are learning the same game, but each table has a slightly different set of rules. This is the hidden element in BARNGA.

Learn the game. Ask participants to help the other members of their group learn the game. Encourage the groups to play a few practice rounds. When participants have had sufficient practice, take away their handouts.

Conduct Round 1. This round consists of local tournaments at each table. Ask participants to play silently for 5 minutes. They should keep track of the number of tricks won by each partnership. During the tournament, participants may not talk or write notes to each other. (However, they may gesture and draw pictures to settle any disagreements.) After 5 minutes, identify the winning partners at each table.

Conduct Round 2. During this round, the winning partners advance to the next table. The partnerships at each table will now try to use different rules, creating chaos and confusion. Continue to prohibit all verbal communication. Encourage participants to solve their problems through gestures and drawings. After 5 minutes, identify the winning partners at each table.

Conduct Round 3. During this round, the winners advance to the next table and then switch partners. During the round, partners have difficulties communicating with each other and presenting a common front to their opponents. Once again, prohibit verbal communication. After 5 minutes, identify the winning partners at each table.

Debrief the participants. Bring the activity to a close. Follow up with a debriefing session.

Differences from the Previous Version

If you are familiar with the previous version of BARNGA (published by Intercultural Press), here are brief descriptions of key changes.

Improved card game. FIVE TRICKS, the card game incorporated in this version of BARNGA, has a new twist: Four cards are put aside during each deal, increasing the chance element in the game. This encourages participants with limited previous experience with card games.

Systematic differences in the rules. The differences between the rules of FIVE TRICKS at one table and the next are adjusted, play-tested, and revised. The current differences provide an optimal jolt to the players.

Standard size for play groups. In this version, the FIVE TRICKS game is always played among four people. This avoids unnecessary confusion when moving people from one table to another.

Partnership play. FIVE TRICKS involves two partnerships. This arrangement enables players to reflect on the impact of the moral support provided by partnerships.

Standard handout format. Instructions for playing different versions of FIVE TRICKS are now of the same length and have the same side headings. This identical appearance strengthens participants' mistaken assumption that everyone is playing by the same rules.

A little piece of misdirection. The ten different handouts now contain an identical "typographical error." The facilitator points this out while participants are learning the game. This incidental byplay provides a subliminal suggestion that all the rules are exactly the same.

Different tournament formats. During Round 2, the winning partners stay together. During Round 3, partnerships are switched. This raises some new types of communication problems and issues related to changing loyalties.

Expanded debriefing section. This section incorporates the field-tested six-step model for debriefing and presents several suggested questions for discussion.

How to Get Ready to Conduct BARNGA

Spend some time becoming familiar with BARNGA and preparing to conduct it. Here are some suggestions:

Learn the Game

The first step in conducting BARNGA is learning the game. The best way to do this is to be a participant or a co-facilitator when an experienced facilitator conducts the game. If you don't have this opportunity, read the next section of this booklet carefully and review the other sections. As you read, visualize conducting the game with a group of participants. Underline or highlight critical activities. Scribble notes to yourself in the margins. Become familiar with the mechanics of the game, but don't try to memorize the rules. Remember that you must not explain all the rules of the game at the beginning. You will have plenty of free time during the game while the players are busy. At that time, you can review the next set of instructions and get ready for the next round of the game.

Make Adjustments

Read the chapter titled How to Modify BARNGA. Depending on your needs and constraints, make appropriate changes to the game. Record the changes in this booklet.

Prepare Rule Summaries

While briefing the players and explaining the rules of the game, it is a good idea to use suitable summary charts that outline the major points. These summaries focus participants' attention and provide a checklist to ensure that you don't forget anything important. Use the reproducible masters on the last ten pages of the book. Copy these pages on blank acetate sheets to make transparencies. If you prefer, you can easily create PowerPoint® slides by typing the content onto bullet slides. Alternatively, you can copy the contents of each transparency master to a page of your flip chart.

Prepare Handouts

BARNGA incorporates a card game called FIVE TRICKS. Participants learn the rules of this game by reading individual copies of a handout.

Prepare a different set of handouts for each group of four participants. The key element in BARNGA is that the rules for FIVE TRICKS are slightly different from one set of the handouts to the next. These differences involve

- value of aces (high or low)
- presence of trumps (no trumps, spades as trumps, or diamonds as trumps)
- use of trumps (only when the player cannot follow suit or at any time)

The differences among the rules of the ten versions are shown in this table.

Table 3.1

Version	Ace	Trump	Trump any time?
1	High	No	—
2	High	Spades	No
3	Low	Spades	No
4	Low	Spades	Yes
5	High	Spades	Yes
6	High	Diamonds	Yes
7	Low	Diamonds	Yes
8	Low	Diamonds	No
9	High	Diamonds	No
10	Low	No	—

Participants should not be aware that the handouts at one table are different from the handouts at another table. Do not copy different sets of handouts on paper of different colors. Since all the handouts are designed to look alike, it is important for you not to get them mixed up.

Here is how you keep the handouts separate. Each version of the handout is identified by a secret code. If you check the lower right corner of each handout page, you will see a picture of a hand of playing cards. The card on top of this picture indicates the version of the handout: If this card is an ace, the handout is the first one; if the card is a 2, the handout is the second one, and so on.

Make four copies of the first handout. Put these copies in a folder and label the folder "Table 1." Make four copies of the second handout, and put them in a folder labeled "Table 2." Repeat the process until you have enough sets of handouts for your participants.

Collect Required Supplies

Playing cards. You need a deck of playing cards for each group of four players. Actually, you need only 24 cards (Ace through 6) for each group, but it is better to give them complete decks and let participants remove the unnecessary cards.

Paper and pencil. At each table place a pad of paper and a pen (or a pencil). Ask players to use these supplies for keeping score.

Projector and screen. Use an overhead projector or a computer and an LCD projector for displaying rule summaries. If these devices are not available, use a flip chart (or large sheets of newsprint paper) with the rule summaries.

Flip chart and markers. Even if you are using projectors, you will still need a flip chart for use during debriefing. Make sure that you have plenty of blank pages.

Whistle. You need some type of attention-getting device (a bell, a siren, or a buzzer) to interrupt busy interaction among participants and move them to the next round of the game. After testing several noise makers, I have selected a wooden whistle that sounds like a train whistle. This device produces the least jarring and the most pleasant sound that is easily recognized in different parts of the world.

Timer. Use a countdown timer for implementing time limits for each round of play. Most digital wristwatches now have a built-in timer. You can also purchase inexpensive electronic timers from kitchen-supply stores. I use a software program with a countdown timer that can be projected on a screen through an LCD projector.

Set Up the Tables

Set up a round table (or a card table) with four chairs around it for each group of four players. If you are working in a hotel meeting room, ask for "cocktail tables" (which are smaller) instead of the usual banquet tables. Set the tables up as far apart from each other as possible. Place a sign holder or a large tent card on table. Mark the table with an identifying number, beginning with 1 and proceeding sequentially.

In addition to the sign with the table number, make sure that each table contains a folder with the appropriate set of rules, a deck of cards, a score pad, and pencils. Make sure that the version number of the handouts at each table matches the table number.

Plan and Rehearse

Plan the briefing procedure: Decide how you want to introduce the rules of the game. Select and arrange the transparencies, and walk through the outline.

Plan your debriefing procedure: Study the debriefing section and select the discussion questions you want to use. If you prefer, you may prepare a handout listing these questions or copy them on flip chart pages.

If you are planning to work with a co-facilitator, work out details of the division of labor and rehearse the flow of the game. Anticipate possible disasters and work out suitable contingency plans.

Don't brood too long on disaster scenarios, however. Visualize your participants enjoying and learning from playing BARNGA. Get ready to enjoy your role as a facilitator.

How to Conduct BARNGA

Skim through the table below to get a feel for the flow of BARNGA. This table provides a preview of what happens during the simulation game, along with approximate time requirements.

Table 4.1

Step	Time	Activity
Conduct Preliminary Activities	3 minutes	Organize participants into groups of four. Ask participants to locate the handouts and the deck of playing cards.
Learn FIVE TRICKS	4 minutes	Ask participants to learn the card game from the handout and play a few practice games.
Conduct the First Round	5 minutes	Ask groups at each table to silently play FIVE TRICKS for 5 minutes and to keep score.
Coordinate the First Transition	2 minutes	Send the winning partners at each table to the next table.
Conduct the Second Round	5 minutes	Ask the groups to silently play FIVE TRICKS for 5 minutes. When problems arise because of different rules, ask participants to negotiate nonverbally.
Coordinate the Second Transition	2 minutes	Send the winning partners at each table to the next table. Ask them to switch partners.

(continued)

Table 4.1 (continued)

Step	Time	Activity
Conduct the Third Round	5 minutes	Ask the groups to silently play FIVE TRICKS for 5 minutes. When problems arise because of different rules, ask participants to negotiate nonverbally.
Conclude the Session	2 minutes	Bring the activity to a close and get ready for a debriefing discussion.

Detailed instructions for conducting each step of BARNGA are given below.

Conduct Preliminary Activities

Brief participants. Welcome all participants. Display Transparency 1. Explain that participants are going to learn a card game called FIVE TRICKS. Do not reveal that the activity explores cross-cultural communication. Instead, position the activity as a preliminary simulation of how participants with different learning styles can learn a cooperative setting and play it in a competitive setting.

Organize participants. Display Transparency 2. Divide participants into groups of four and seat each group around a table. Ask leftover participants to become Game Wardens and help you conduct the game. Assign the Game Wardens to different tables and ask them to make sure that your instructions are correctly carried out.

Distribute play materials. Ask groups at each table to pick up the folder with handouts and distribute one copy to each player. Also ask each group to pick up the deck of playing cards and remove the cards that are not required during the play of the game.

Learn FIVE TRICKS

Ask the groups to learn FIVE TRICKS. Project Transparency 3. Tell the four players at each table to read the handout, choose partners, and cooperatively figure out how to play the card game.

Announce a "correction." While participants are reviewing the handout, pretend to notice a typographical error. Blow a whistle to get participants' attention and make an announcement similar to this:

> *I've noticed a typo in your rule sheet. Let's get it corrected.*
>
> *Please locate the second line of the paragraph with the side heading "Winning Tricks." It reads, "The person who played this card gathers up the trick and places it face in front of him or her." It should read, ". . . places it face down in front of him or her."*
>
> *Please make this correction now.*

This incidental business subtly suggests to participants that they all have identical sets of rules.

Encourage practice play. Suggest that the groups play FIVE TRICKS with the cards face up to help everyone master the mechanics and strategy of the game.

Take away the handouts. After a few minutes of practice, ask participants at each table to place their handouts inside the folder. Ask the groups to continue playing the game without referring to the handouts. While participants continue playing, collect the handout folders from each table.

Conduct Round 1

Impose a gag order. Blow the whistle and project Transparency 4. Ask the groups to continue playing FIVE TRICKS, without talking to each other. If they need to communicate with each other, they should do so nonverbally (through gestures and grunts). They may also draw pictures, but may not write any words.

Start the first round. Blow the whistle to interrupt the game. Project Transparency 5. Ask each group to start a new game of FIVE TRICKS and play silently. One player at each table should keep score by recording the number of tricks won by the partnerships at the end of each game. After each game, the players should immediately start a new one. They should continue playing one game after another for the next 5 minutes.

Monitor the play. Start your timer and observe the groups. Enforce the gag order by firmly asking any outlaws to stop talking. If you have any Game Wardens, call them to the front of the room (and out of earshot of the players) and explain what is going to happen during the next round.

Coordinate the First Transition

Stop the game. At the end of 5 minutes, blow the whistle and ask participants to stop the game immediately. Ask the scorekeeper at each table to record the number of tricks won by each partnership in this partial game.

Identify the winning partners. Ask participants at each table to total their tricks and to find out which partnership won the most tricks. If there is a tie at any table, arbitrarily point to one partnership and declare them winners. Ask the winning partners to stand up.

Shift the players. Announce that the winning partnerships will be promoted to a different table for tournament play. Ask each pair of winning partners to move to the next table. (The winners at the last table should move to the first one.)

Conduct the Second Round

Start the tournament. Ask the winning partners to shake hands with the players already at the table. Ask the groups to begin playing FIVE TRICKS for the next 5 minutes. Project Transparency 5 again and remind the players that the gag order is still in effect. Ask one player at each table keep score as before.

Do not interfere. Sooner or later, the players will reach a state of chaos and confusion because of the differences in the two sets of rules operating at each table. If any player asks you for clarification, simply shrug your shoulders and tell the group to do the best they can through nonverbal communication. Encourage the teams to quickly settle their disputes and to continue playing.

Coordinate the Second Transition

Stop the game. At the end of 5 minutes, blow the whistle to interrupt the game. Ask the scorekeeper at each table to record the number of tricks won by each partnership during the last game.

Identify the winning partners. Ask participants at each table to total their tricks and to find out which partnership won the most tricks. If there is a tie at any table, arbitrarily point to one partnership and declare them winners. Ask the winning partners to stand up.

Shift the players. Inform participants that the winning partners will be sent to a different table. Ask each pair of winning partners to move to the next table. The winners at the last table should move to the first one.

Switch partners. After the winning partners have seated themselves at the new table, project Transparency 5. Tell the players to switch partners (so that each new-comer to the table will be partnering with an old-timer at the table). Help the groups make this switch.

Conduct the Third Round

Start the next tournament. Blow the whistle and ask the groups to begin playing FIVE TRICKS for the next 5 minutes. Remind them of the gag order and the scorekeeping procedure.

Monitor the play. As before, leave the players to their own devices. Make a note of any interesting incidents that should be discussed during the debriefing session.

Conclude the Session

Announce the end of the tournament. After 5 minutes, blow the whistle to interrupt the play. Ask the scorekeeper at each table to record the number of tricks won by each partnership in the last game.

Identify the winning partners. Use the same procedure as before. However, in case of ties, ask both pairs of partners to stand up. Congratulate the winners and lead a round of applause.

Send participants to the home table. Ask participants to put away the decks of playing cards and return to their original tables where they first learned to play FIVE TRICKS. Announce the removal of the gag order and encourage participants to talk to each other. Wait patiently for the excited conversations to wind down.

Get ready for debriefing. Remember that the most important phase of BARNGA is yet to come. Review the instructions for the debriefing session while participants are talking to each other.

How to Debrief BARNGA Players

Debriefing is a discussion that is conducted after the play of a simulation game. It helps participants to reflect on their experience, relate it to the real world, discover useful insights, and share them with each other.

True learning comes from a combination of action and learning. To gain maximum learning from an experiential activity, it is very important for you to set aside enough time for debriefing and to facilitate this process in a systematic (yet flexible) fashion. Skipping the debriefing activity is unwise at best and unprofessional at worst. Without debriefing, some players may feel happy and excited, others may feel confused, frustrated, or upset, and most will be left wondering, "What was it all about?" Debriefing will help you to reduce negative reactions, bring the game to a close, and increase useful insights. There are many (including me) who believe that debriefing is more important than the original play and the simulation game is merely an excuse for the debriefing discussion.

Structure and Spontaneity

In conducting the debriefing session, you face a major dilemma between structure and spontaneity. This chapter provides you with a structured set of guidelines and suggested questions based on a six-phase model for debriefing. However, during actual debriefing, you should go with the flow and encourage spontaneous comments from participants. The debriefing model is merely a safety net: If the conversation degenerates into a rambling dialogue, return to the appropriate phase of debriefing and use the list of ready-made questions. At other times, however, let the discussion proceed in its natural course. Do not discourage participants by reacting to comments with such statements as, "We will be talking about that in Phase 5. We are now only in Phase 2. So please hold your thought until later." Remember that you can always return to a previous phase of debriefing later.

Here is a preview of the six phases of structured debriefing; each phase is identified by a key question:

- **Phase 1.** How do you feel? This phase gives the players an opportunity to express their feelings and emotions so they can be more objective during the later phases.
- **Phase 2.** What happened? This phase compares and contrasts different players' experiences in BARNGA and identifies patterns of behaviors during the play of the game.
- **Phase 3.** What did you learn? This phase discusses general principles and insights from playing BARNGA.
- **Phase 4.** How does this relate? This phase examines the relevance of BARNGA to real-world situations.
- **Phase 5.** What if? This phase speculates about possible consequences of changing the context and rules of playing BARNGA.
- **Phase 6.** What next? This phase involves action planning based on insights gained from BARNGA.

Here are specific suggestions for conducting each of these phases.

Phase 1. How Do You Feel?

Explain the purpose of this phase: It gives participants an opportunity to vent their feelings about BARNGA. This phase makes it easier for participants to conduct an objective discussion during the later phases of debriefing.

Begin with these questions:

How did you feel about playing BARNGA?
How do you feel about its outcomes?

Invite participants to get in touch with their feelings. Point out that it is often difficult to reflect and talk at the same time. Observe a couple of minutes of silence to permit people to reflect on their emotional reactions to the play of BARNGA and its outcomes.

Invite participants to share their feelings. Encourage (but don't force) participants to express their feelings. Whenever a participant talks, ask others to listen in a nonjudgmental fashion.

Postpone intense conversations. While it is important for you to encourage free expression of emotions and feelings, make sure that this phase does not become a therapy session. If some overwhelmed participant has emotional needs beyond what can be met immediately, suggest an individual session at a later time.

Ask questions about different roles. Name each of these roles and ask participants to report their feelings toward the person in that role:

- Facilitator
- Partner
- Opponents during Round 1 (who played by the same rules)
- Opponents during Round 2 (who played by a different set of rules)
- Partners during Round 3 (who played by a different set of rules)
- Players at other tables

Suggest different feelings. Ask participants if they experienced these feelings during the play of BARNGA. Ask for specific details of what happened to cause these feelings:

- Anxiety
- Fear
- Friendliness
- Frustration
- Happiness
- Paranoia
- Satisfaction
- Stupidity
- Suspicion
- Sympathy
- Tension

Phase 2. What Happened?

Explain the purpose of this phase: You are collecting data from different participants about their experiences during the play of BARNGA. This phase makes it possible for participants to compare and contrast their recollections and to draw some general conclusions.

Begin this phase with this broad question:

What important things happened during the game?

Follow up by using other adjectives:

What surprising things happened during the game?
What amusing things happened during the game?
What stressful things happened during the game?

Follow up with questions about specific events. Identify each event from the following list, and then ask participants to recall what happened during that event:

- Team formation
- Facilitator's correction of the typographical error in the handout
- Learning FIVE TRICKS
- Practice play of FIVE TRICKS
- Competitive play during Round 1
- Being sent to the next table for Round 2
- Being left behind at the same table during Round 2
- Noticing "incorrect" play by the other players for the first time
- Trying to communicate nonverbally
- Agreeing on a new set of rules
- Conclusion of Round 2
- Switching partners in Round 3
- Conclusion of the session

Phase 3. What Did You Learn?

Explain the purpose of this phase: It encourages participants to state and to test different principles based on their play of BARNGA.

Ask participants to share the principles they discovered. Give an example, if necessary: *Always check your assumptions.*

Discuss the validity of each principle. Ask participants whether the principle should be accepted, rejected, or modified. Encourage participants to provide data from the play of the BARNGA and from real-world experiences to back up their opinions. Encourage open discussion and inquiry.

Use this list of principles. These are principles suggested by earlier participants in BARNGA sessions. Many of them may be rediscovered by your participants. If there are long periods of silence during this phase, select and present some principles from this list to keep the discussion going.

- In most interpersonal situations, we make several unwarranted assumptions.
- People engaged in the same activity may use different procedures.
- Not everyone may have the same set of rules.
- You can't believe everything you read.
- Communication problems exacerbate cross-cultural clashes.
- People with nonverbal communication skills have an advantage.
- Having a partner reduces the impact of a culture shock.
- People look for outside guidance and help during chaotic situations.
- During chaotic situations people tend to blame the "others."
- In chaotic situations, unscrupulous people implement or make up rules that give them an advantage.
- Assertive people have an advantage.
- When other people behave differently from your expectations, you assume that they are dishonest or ignorant.
- Very few people consider the possibility that different people may have different rules.
- Whenever you learn a standard set of rules, you feel that they are the only correct set of rules.
- In a conflict situation, some people give up easily rather than explain their views.
- Some people are too embarrassed to communicate in unconventional ways.
- Different folks may have different strokes.
- The home team has an advantage in being able to impose its rules on people coming from the outside.
- After being through a culture shock, people find it easier to accept further shocks.
- People prefer opponents who play by the same rules to partners who play by different rules.

Phase 4. How Does This Relate to the Real World?

Explain the purpose of this phase: It deals with the relevance of BARNGA to participants' real-world environment.

Ask participants to suggest everyday analogies. Also, suggest that BARNGA is a metaphor for some real-world event, and ask participants to speculate on what those events might be.

Present specific events from the simulation game. Use the list under Phase 2 and ask the players to come up with similar incidents from their workplace.

Relate different objects and procedures. Use the following list and ask participants to identify analogies in their workplace.

- FIVE TRICKS card game
- Handouts
- Players' tables
- Score sheets
- Gag order
- Switching partners
- Being left behind

Relate specific roles. Use the list under Phase 1. Ask participants to identify similar people and roles in their organization.

Relate specific principles. Use the list from Phase 3. Ask participants to relate each principle to their workplace experiences.

Phase 5. What If?

Explain the purpose of this phase: It helps participants to speculate on alternative scenarios and to extrapolate the principles they discovered.

Present suggested scenarios. Use the items from the following list. Ask participants to suggest how it would have affected their behaviors during the play of BARNGA. Later, invite participants to present their own what-if scenarios.

- At the beginning of the session, participants are told that the rules of FIVE TRICKS are different at different tables.
- Participants are allowed to speak throughout the play of FIVE TRICKS.

- Partners are permitted to communicate with each other through notes, but they are not permitted to communicate with their opponents.
- A more complex card game (such as BRIDGE) is used instead of FIVE TRICKS.
- The winning partners receive a cash prize at the end of each round.
- FIVE TRICKS is played by individuals instead of partners.
- Partners spend 30 minutes playing the initial round of FIVE TRICKS.
- Each round of FIVE TRICKS lasts for 30 minutes.
- Before the game, some participants are warned that their opponents might cheat.
- Two more rounds of the FIVE TRICKS tournaments are played.

Phase 6. What Next?

Explain the purpose of this phase: It gives an opportunity to plan suitable strategies for replaying BARNGA—and for better communication in the workplace.

Ask for improved BARNGA strategies. Use these open-ended questions:

> *If we played BARNGA again with a new group, how would you behave differently—knowing what you know now?*

> *What advice would you give to a friend who is about to play BARNGA for the first time?*

Follow up with real-world action planning. Ask this question:

> *How will your workplace behavior change as a result of the insights gained from playing BARNGA?*

Reminder

Remember that the debriefing phases and questions are presented as flexible suggestions and not as rigid requirements. Feel free to skip phases, ignore questions, return to previous phases, and rearrange the sequence. Don't be alarmed if the discussion jumps from one phase to another and revisits an earlier phase. As long as the important points are covered in the debriefing session, you have achieved your purpose.

How to Use Games for Debriefing BARNGA

The debriefing session that follows the play of BARNGA frequently turns out to be anticlimactic. Earlier, during the play of the simulation game, everyone is enthusiastic and excited. Now, during the debriefing, they become somber and slightly bored.

My friend Roger Greenaway has spent several decades exploring the debriefing process and coming up with brilliant ideas about how to make them more effective and engaging. Visit his website (http://reviewing.co.uk/) for a collection of his articles and ideas about debriefing. One of Roger's wishes is that the debriefing session should be as interesting as the earlier simulation game. I agree with him and I have designed a series of debriefing games to meet this goal. Here are two such games that I use to follow up the play of BARNGA.

1. Artful Lesson

This activity begins with reflection, proceeds through nonverbal communication, and ends in a discussion.

Time

15 to 30 minutes

Supplies

- Large sheets of drawing paper
- Crayons of different colors
- Timer
- Whistle

Flow

Stay in teams. Make sure that participants are still seated in play groups of four around tables. If you had some observers who did not play BARNGA earlier, add them to different tables.

Review the experience. Ask participants to silently think back on what happened during the play of BARNGA. Invite them to close their eyes and visualize the highlights of the event. After a suitable pause, ask participants to silently focus on one or more lessons they learned from the experience.

Distribute supplies. Place sheets of drawing paper and boxes of crayons in the middle of each table. Ask each participant to take a sheet of paper and to share the crayons.

Time to draw. Invite participants to draw an abstract picture that captures the lessons they learned from BARNGA. Discourage them from worrying about the artistic quality of the picture and encourage them to capture their intuitive thoughts and feelings. Announce a 5-minute time limit for this activity.

Time to stop. At the end of 5 minutes, blow the whistle and ask participant-artists to stop drawing. Reassure them that it does not matter if their picture is not yet complete.

Interpret other people's pictures. At each table, ask participants to take turns holding up their pictures. While doing this, ask each person to perform the difficult task of keeping his or her mouth shut. Invite other participants around the table to treat the picture as a Rorschach inkblot and report what they see in it. It is not necessary that participants take turns in presenting their interpretation. Anyone may call out an interpretation at any time.

Interpret your own picture. After all pictures have been interpreted, ask the table teams to repeat the process. This time, however, each artist should hold up the picture and describe what lesson he or she meant to convey.

Discussion

After sharing insights, encourage a discussion at each table. Use questions similar to these to structure this discussion.

- What lessons were the most frequently mentioned?
- What lessons were unexpected and unique?
- What was the most powerful lesson that affected you?
- How do you expect this lesson to change your future behavior?

2. THIRTY-FIVE

THIRTY-FIVE is one of my favorite debriefing games. In this activity, participants reflect on what happened during the play of BARNGA and identify important practical lessons they learned. They write one of these lessons as a brief item. The winner in this activity is *not* the best player, but the best practical lesson.

Time

15 to 30 minutes

Supplies

- Index cards
- Whistle

Flow

Brief participants. Ask participants to think back on their experiences and observations during the play of BARNGA. Ask participants to write down a practical guideline they learned from the simulation game on an index card. Give an example (*If rules are violated, do not immediately assume that somebody is making a mistake.*) to illustrate a practical guidelines. Instruct participants to keep their guidelines short, specific, clear, and legible. Announce a 2-minute time limit.

Let go. After 2 minutes, blow the whistle and give instructions for getting ready for the next activity. Ask each participant to review the guideline on the card, emotionally detach himself or herself from it, and get ready to launch it into the world.

Switch guidelines. Ask participants to turn their cards face down to hide the guidelines. When you blow the whistle, participants are to stand up, walk around, and exchange the cards with each other. Participants should not read the guidelines on the cards but should immediately exchange it with someone else. They should continue doing this until you blow the whistle again.

Find a partner. Blow the whistle to begin the exchange process. After about 20 seconds, blow the whistle again to stop the process. Ask participants to stop moving and to pair up with any nearby participant.

Compare and score. Ask each pair of participants to review the two guidelines on the two cards they have. They should distribute seven points between these two guidelines (no fractions or negative numbers) to reflect their relative merit. Participants should write these numbers on the back of the cards.

Conduct the second round. After a suitable pause for scoring, blow the whistle again and ask participants to repeat the process of moving around and exchanging cards. When you blow the whistle again after 20 seconds or so, participants stop moving, find a partner, compare the two guidelines on their cards, and distribute seven points. The new score points should be written below the previous ones.

Conduct three more rounds. Tell participants that you will be conducting three more rounds of the activity. Suggest to participants that they should maintain high levels of objectivity by disregarding earlier numbers and by keeping a poker face if they end up with the guidelines they themselves wrote.

Count down to the winning guidelines. At the end of the fifth round, ask participants to return to their seats with the card they currently have. Ask them to add the five score points and write the total. After a suitable pause, count down from 35. When a participant hears the total on the card, he or she should stand up and read the item on the card.

Discuss the guideline. When someone reads the first guideline, lead a round of applause. Briefly comment on the guideline and invite other participants to make their comments.

Continue the countdown. Continue from where you left off previously. Identify more guidelines, listen and applaud, and hold a brief discussion. Continue the countdown procedure until you have identified the top ten guidelines.

Follow up. Thank participants for generating the practical guidelines and evaluating them. Tell them that you will type up a complete set of guidelines and distribute them either through regular mail or e-mail. (Be sure to follow up on this promise!)

How to Use BARNGA for Alternative Purposes

Although BARNGA is primarily referred to as a simulation game that deals with cross-cultural communication, it can be used to explore communication among people who have different kinds of differences. Within the broad topic of communication, we have used BARNGA to train participants in these areas of human differences:

- Nationality (Example: U.S. vs. Canadian)
- National origin (Example: African vs. European)
- First language (Example: Spanish vs. Bengali)
- Religion (Example: Jewish vs. Moslem)
- Political beliefs (Example: conservative vs. liberal)
- Socioeconomic (Example: rich vs. poor)
- Profession (Example: engineers vs. salespeople)
- Organization (Example: large vs. small)
- Age (Example: baby boomers vs. generation Xers)
- Birth order (Example: first born vs. middle)
- Marital status (Example: married vs. divorced)
- Reading interests (Example: mysteries vs. science fiction)
- Personal characteristics (Example: optimist vs. pessimist)
- Personality type (Example: introvert vs. extrovert)
- Thinking style (Example: analytical vs. global)
- Learning style (Example: visual vs. auditory)

In using BARNGA to explore these differences, the game usually does not have to be altered significantly. But the debriefing questions should emphasize the selected areas of difference.

Gender Differences

One specific topic in which we have effectively used BARNGA is gender differences in communication styles. For maximum impact, a large group with equal numbers of men and women is desirable. Here's what happened during a recent play of BARNGA.

1. We started the activity with two play groups, each exclusively of men and women.

2. After learning and practicing the game in same-gender groups, participants formed mixed-gender groups for the second round. At each table, each pair of partners were of the same gender and so the game became a contest between the sexes.

3. Another interesting change occured during the third round. By switching partners, we made it necessary for people of opposite genders to cooperate with each other (and to compete against the other mixed pair).

As you can imagine, behaviors from this type of play yielded a lot of interesting issues and insights for the debriefing discussion. By the way, when we do not have conveniently equal numbers of men and women, we organize as many same-gender groups as possible. The rest play in mixed-gender groups.

Mergers and Acquisitions

We are frequently hired to conduct team-building activities for employees of two (or more) corporations that have recently merged with each other. BARNGA becomes an effective tool in these situations. Here's how we use BARNGA in merger interventions:

1. We organize each play group to include employees from the same parent organization. We seat the play groups alternating the organizations: The first table seats employees of Company A, the second table seats employees of Company B, the third table seats Company A, the fourth table seats company B, and so on.

2. We conduct the learning, practice, and first-round sessions with these intact play groups.

3. During the first transition, when the winners move to the next table, we end up with merged groups incorporating partners from different organizations.

4. Immediately after the end of the second round, we conduct a debriefing session. We draw a parallel between what happened during the game (due to differences in the rules) and what is happening in the mergered organization (due to the differences in policies and procedures). We brainstorm appropriate strategies for reducing and removing dysfunctional clashes among employees from different organizations.

5. After the debriefing session, we coordinate the second transition. At the new tables, we ask participants to change partners (reflecting working with new colleagues), remove the gag order, and ask them to conduct a new tournament. Almost invariably, before beginning the rounds, players spontaneously identify differences in the rules and agree upon a set of rules that are acceptable to everyone.

6. At the end of the round, we conduct the final debriefing session in which we stress the importance of identifying and reconciling differences among explicit and implicit procedures that create chaos and confusion. We spend time identifying one or two major policy differences and work out collaborative revisions.

Cross-Functional Teamwork

When we help our clients with corporate reorgnization efforts, a frequent goal is to remove the traditional separation among different departments (such as design, production, marketing, customer support, and human resources) and to create new cross-functional working relationships. In these situations, we use BARNGA in the way described above in reference to corporate mergers: We begin with intact play groups with participants from the same departments and mix them between one round and the next. When this is not possible (because of unequal representation from different departments), we try to create as many intact groups as possible. During the debriefing session, we relate the inefficiencies associated with playing by different rules to what is happening when departmental boundaries are strictly enforced. We also discuss the importance of identifying and flexibly changing the clashing rules when cross-functional work procedures are created.

Change Management

In one sense, BARNGA is all about change management: how people react to sudden and unexpected changes, especially when there is little or no communication.

We have frequently used this simulation game in change-management workshops. This is how we do it:

1. We conduct a debriefing session immediately at the end of the second round (when participants have completed playing under different and unclear rules). We elicit and discuss negative reactions associated with the surprise and confusion. We relate these reactions to what happens during organizational change. We brainstorm strategies for reducing and removing the undesirable surprise and confusion, both in the game and in the workplace.

2. After moving the winners to the next table and before playing the next round, we remove the gag order. During the final debriefing session, we ask participants to recall what they talked about before and during play and how these conversations helped them. We use this discussion to generate a set of guidelines for effectively coping with organizational change.

Creative Problem Solving

One of the major outcomes of playing BARNGA is an increased awareness of the assumptions that we make and maintain. In our training workshops on creative problem solving, we play BARNGA under the name of CYA. This acronym stands for *Check Your Assumptions* (and not for what you assumed).

In CYA, we conduct a debriefing discussion at the end of the second round (after participants have confronted unexpected rule differences). During this discussion, we focus on

- the assumption we made (Everybody's playing by the same rules.)
- the reason for this assumption (Everybody is using the same materials.)
- how we maintained the assumption (The other partners must have misunderstood the rules.)

We also point out our tendency to blame the others (and ourselves) rather than examine the system.

During the next round (at a new table and with changed partners), we ask participants to continue playing the game silently. We invite them to creatively handle rule differences using unconventional modes of communication. During the final debriefing discussion, we stress the importance of

- keeping an open mind
- mindfully observing what is happening
- focusing on solving the problem rather than blaming each other

Communication Skills

Much of the frustration in BARNGA arises from a lack of communication. In a special version of BARNGA, we permit controlled types of written communication (to reflect heavy use of e-mail in organizations). This is how it works:

1. During the second round of play (when participants confront unexpected rule changes), we permit partners to write notes to each other. Usually, partners comment on strange happenings, make snide remarks about the other pair, and come up with suggestions for imposing the "correct" rules. Sometimes, a participant may realize that the rules are different and share this discovery with the partner.
2. At the end of the round, we collect the notes from each table and continue with the transition and the play of the next round.
3. During this round, we permit participants to write notes to anyone else at the table and even display the same note to all players. At the end of the round, we collect the notes from the table.
4. During the debriefing discussion, we end up with interesting data in the form of notes written by different players. We select and read some of the notes anonymously and use the information to track what happened during the moments of confusion and during attempts at bringing some semblance of order to the situation.

Negotiation Skills

We have used BARNGA to provide appropriate practice in negotiation and persuasion skills. This is how we do it:

1. At the end of the second round, we point out to participants that they have been playing the card game by different rules. We briefly recap the differences between the rules and ask players at each table to collaboratively agree on a set of rules they want to use for the next round of play. While play groups are discussing the rules, we roam around and collect information about their negotiation behaviors.

2. After the groups have agreed on the preferred set of rules, we ask participants to mingle with others and find a partner from a different table. Each participant now attempts to persuade the other participant to accept the version of the rules agreed upon at his or her table. Once again, we collect information about negotiation styles.

3. We reassemble all participants and conduct a debriefing session about effective and ineffective negotiation strategies.

Additional Uses

As an experiential strategy, BARNGA deals with the impact of differences among people. This basic element is true of many aspects of human interaction. Therefore, you can use BARNGA for exploring topics that involve interaction among people who are different from each other in one aspect or another. In addition to the alternative uses described above, we have used BARNGA to explore such training topics as leadership, delegation, coaching, collaborative planning, customer service, and project management.

Experiment with your own alternative applications of BARNGA. Make minor adjustments to the rules and major adjustments to debriefing questions. Try out your game with a typical group and make additional adjustments based on the feedback from participants.

You will find that playing with BARNGA could be as exciting as playing BARNGA.

How to Modify BARNGA

I designed BARNGA for maximum flexibility so that you can easily modify it to suit the constraints and resources in your situation.

Non English-Speaking Participants

BARNGA has been used around the world with participants who do not speak or read English. If you are in this situation, we are making the assumption that you (the facilitator) are bilingual in both English and the participants' first language. As a part of getting ready for BARNGA, translate the appropriate versions of the FIVE TRICKS rules into the local language. My friends have already done this if your participants' first language is French, German, or Spanish. You can select the appropriate rule sets from the back of the book and make photocopies. With other languages, you have to undertake your own translations and make photocopies of local language versions.

Number of Participants

The ideal number of players for BARNGA is 16 to 24, divided into four to six play groups. These numbers ensure increased probability that participants will experience a different version of the rules during each round. However, you may not always have the ideal number of participants. Here are some suggestions for handling different numbers of participants.

Odd Numbers

If the number of participants is not evenly divisible by four and you end up with one to three people left over, give the extra participants the role of *Game Wardens* and ask them to help you conduct the game. While the groups are busy playing

FIVE TRICKS during the first round, assemble the Game Wardens in a convenient corner and explain the secret of different rules at different tables. Ask the Game Wardens to observe how participants react to the rule differences during the next round.

Large Number of Participants

I have played BARNGA with more than 200 participants at the same time. The good news about such large groups is that they create contagious excitement and enthusiasm. If the audience trusts you and likes you, participants will quiet disruptive people and ensure that everybody follows the rules. The bad news, on the other hand, is that if the audience doesn't trust you or like you, participants will gang up and give you a hard time. Also with large groups, things appear to move in slow motion: Distributing play materials, explaining the rules, and the transition from one round to the next take a lot more time.

Here's how I handle large groups: I divide participants into groups of five (instead of the usual groups of four). In each group, I ask for a volunteer to act as the non-playing Game Warden. One of the important tasks for the Game Wardens is to listen to your instructions and make sure that the players in their groups follow them. You can assemble the Game Wardens in front of the room while the others are busy playing each round of FIVE TRICKS to explain what is going to happen during the next round.

The Game Wardens can also observe and record interesting behaviors and conversations in their play groups. This information becomes valuable raw material during the debriefing discussion. Game Wardens can also coordinate debriefing discussions among the players at their table.

Emphasize to the Game Wardens that they should not interfere with the play of BARNGA except to repeat and explain the instructions for each round. They should merely observe and note any "cheating" that takes place at their table. Surprisingly, there is very little resistance from Game Wardens about not being able to participate in the actual play. They feel important about their role, especially when they are entrusted with The Secret. Also, these non-playing members seem to learn the key concepts from BARNGA through vicarious participation.

Small Number of Participants

The minimum number required for BARNGA is 12 (organized into three play groups of four). But I have played BARNGA with fewer participants. The good news about small groups is that it is easier to implement the rules. The bad news is that it makes players more anxious about making mistakes in front of others.

Here are some suggestions for what to do if you end up with small groups of participants:

Four players. Give the first version of the rules (aces high) to two players and the second version (aces low) to the other two. Tell them that they will be partners and send each pair to different corners of the room to study the handout and master the rules. Visit each pair and coach them on the (different) rules for FIVE TRICKS. Then take away the handouts, impose the gag order, and ask participants to play FIVE TRICKS for 5 minutes. Conclude the session after a single round and shift into a debriefing mode. During the discussion, ask what-if questions about three groups and three rounds of play.

Six players. Divide participants into two groups of three. Use the special version of FIVE TRICKS for three players. Reproducible pages for two different versions of rules are printed on the last two pages of this booklet. These rules describe a non-partnership version of the game. In one handout, aces are high; in the other, aces are low.

Eight players. Divide participants into two groups of four. Use the first two versions of the rules. Conclude the session at the end of the second round and shift into the debriefing mode. During the discussion, ask what-if questions about more play groups and another round of play with the switching of partners.

Time Adjustments

BARNGA requires 20 to 30 minutes of play time and an equal amount of time for debriefing. Here are some suggestions on how to speed up the play of the simulation game:

Speed up the learning process. Ask the members of each group to quickly learn the game from their handouts. Don't wait for perfect mastery of the rules; get the first round started as soon as possible.

Skip the first round. As soon as the groups have learned FIVE TRICKS, choose one partnership at each table. Send them to the next table for a tournament. This speeds up the clash among different rules.

Skip the final round. Conclude the activity at the end of the second round. Start the debriefing session immediately.

Play in installments. Schedule four 15-minute sessions on different days. On the first day stop the game at the end of the first round. Conduct the second round on the second day and the third round on the third day. Reserve the fourth day for debriefing.

Here are some suggestions for speeding up the debriefing session:

Small group debriefing. Ask participants to stay in their play groups. Give each group a list of debriefing questions. Ask group members to discuss these questions among themselves. After about 10 minutes, assemble all participants and ask groups to report their major conclusions.

Individual debriefing. Distribute copies of a debriefing questionnaire to participants. Ask each participant to independently think of responses to each question. After about 5 minutes ask participants to pair up with someone else from another play group. Invite these partners to share their responses to the questionnaire.

Journal writing. Begin by stressing the importance of reflecting on the BARNGA experience in order to learn useful principles from it. At some convenient time later during the day, ask participants to write a page or two of a personal journal reflecting their behaviors, reactions, and insights related to the play of BARNGA.

Create Your Own Modifications

One of my favorite sayings about play is

> *Good participants play within the rules; great participants play with the rules.*

Feel free to play with the rules of BARNGA. Experiment with your own variations and enjoy creative design.

What to Do After Playing BARNGA

Although BARNGA can be played as a standalone activity, a more effective approach is to incorporate it as a part of a training workshop. You can also strengthen the impact of BARNGA using various resources.

Books about Differences

BARNGA is primarily about interaction among people who are different from each other. Here are my personal-choice books that deal with three major areas of differences:

Cultural and national differences:

Storti, Craig. (1999) *Figuring Foreigners Out: A Practical Guide.* Boston, MA: Intercultural Press. (ISBN: 1-877864-70-6)

Ting-Toomey, Stella. (1999) *Communicating Across Cultures.* New York, NY: The Guilford Press. (ISBN: 1-57230-445-6)

Gender differences:

Tannen, Deborah. (2001) *You Just Don't Understand: Women and Men in Conversation.* New York, NY: HarperCollins. (ISBN: 0060959622)

Generational differences:

Lancaster, Lynne C. & Stillman, David. (2003) *When Generations Collide: Who They Are. Why They Clash. How to Solve the Generational Puzzle at Work.* New York, NY: HarperCollins. (ISBN: 0066621070)

Books about Training Games and Simulations

BARNGA is a simulation game. Here is a book about different types of training games and simulations:

Thiagarajan, Sivasailam. (2003) *Design Your Own Games and Activities*. San Francisco, CA: Jossey-Bass/Pfeiffer. (ISBN: 0-7879-6465-4)

Conducting BARNGA is not a training activity, but rather a facilitation activity. Here are two books about instructional facilitation (including debriefing):

Luckner, John L. & Nadler, Redlan S. (1997) *Processing the Experience: Strategies to Enhance and Generalize Learning*. Dubuque, IA: Kendall/Hunt Publishing Company. (ISBN 0-7872-1000-5)

Thiagarajan, Sivasailam. (1999) *Facilitator's Toolkit*. Bloomington, IN: Workshops By Thiagi. (ISBN: 1-93005-1506)

Intercultural Training Methods

The best way to train people in intercultural skills and knowledge is by using simulations, training games, and other experiential activities. For an insightful and practical discussion of various methods of intercultural training, read the chapter "An Analysis of Methods for Intercultural Training" by Sandra M. Fowler and Judith M. Blohm in this book:

Landis, Daniel (Editor). (2003) *Handbook of Intercultural Training*. Thousand Oaks, CA: SAGE Publications. (ISBN: 0761923322)

Here are two books that review different cross-cultural training methods:

Fowler, Sandra M. & Mumford, Monica G. (1995) *Intercultural Sourcebook: Cross-Cultural Training Methods (Volume 1)*. Boston, MA: Intercultural Press. (ISBN: 1-877864-29-3)

Fowler, Sandra M. & Mumford, Monica G. (1999) *Intercultural Sourcebook: Cross-Cultural Training Methods (Volume 2)*. Boston, MA: Intercultural Press. (ISBN: 1-877864-64-1)

Books on Intercultural Games and Activities

Here are three books that contain collections of training games and simulations:

Seelye, H. Ned. (1996) *Experiential Activities for Intercultural Learning.* Boston, MA: Intercultural Press. (ISBN: 1-877864-33-1)

Stringer, Donna & Cassiday, Patricia A. (2003) *52 Activities for Exploring Values Differences.* Boston, MA: Intercultural Press. (ISBN: 1-877864-96-x)

Thiagarajan, Sivasailam. (2004) *Simulation Games.* Bloomington, IN: Workshops By Thiagi. (ISBN: 1-93005-1506)

Training Games and Simulations on Diversity

Here are some interactive approaches to intercultural training:

Grove, Cornelius & Hallowell, Willa. (2001) *Randomia Balloon Factory: A Unique Simulation about Working across the Cultural Divide.* Boston, MA: Intercultural Press. (ISBN: 1-877864-92-7)

Nipporica Associates & Saphiere, Dianne Hofner (1997) *Ecotonos: A Multicultural Problem-Solving Simulation.* Boston, MA: Intercultural Press. (ISBN: 1-877864-94-3)

Powers, Richard B. 1999) *An Alien Among Us: A Diversity Game.* Boston, MA: Intercultural Press. (ISBN: 1-877864-74-9)

Shirts, R. Garry. *BaFá BaFá.* Del Mar, CA: Simulation Training Systems.

Shirts, R. Garry. *StarPower.* Del Mar, CA: Simulation Training Systems.

Shirts, R. Garry. *What is No?* Del Mar, CA: Simulation Training Systems.

Professional Organizations

Here are three professional organizations related to simulation gaming and intercultural training (along with their websites):

International Simulation and Gaming Association (ISAGA): *http://www.isaga.info/*

North American Simulation and Gaming Association (NASAGA):
http://nasaga.org/

Society for Intercultural Education, Research and Training (SIETAR):
http://www.sietar.org/

A Special Invitation

Visit my website (www.thiagi.com) for hundreds of free training games, simulations, and facilitation tips. Also, register for my free monthly newsletter.

I have created a special section for BARNGA users as a part of my website. Please contribute modifications that have you made to BARNGA, reports on interesting experiences with this simulation game, and translations of BARNGA rules into different languages.

Reproducible Pages

The following section is printed without page numbers to permit photocopying.

- **English**

  Transparency Masters

  Rules for FIVE TRICKS

  Rules for FIVE TRICKS for Three Players

- **French**

  Transparency Masters

  CINQ PLIS

  CINQ PLIS pour Trois Joueurs

- **German**

  Transparency Masters

  FÜNF STICHE

  FÜNF STICHE für Drei Spieler

- **Spanish**

  Transparency Masters

  CINCO TRUCOS

  CINCO TRUCOS para Tres Jugadores

English

To Explore . . .

- Cooperative learning
- Competitive playing

Instructions

- Form groups of four
- Sit around a table

Learn
FIVE TRICKS

- Read the handout
- Choose your partner

Gag Order

- NO: Talking
- YES: Gestures
- NO: Written words
- YES: Pictures

Tournament

- Play FIVE TRICKS
- Play for 5 minutes
- Play several games
- Keep score

Rules for FIVE TRICKS

Please note:

In all versions of the rules, we have intentionally left out a word in the paragraph with the heading "Winning Tricks."

At the beginning of the game, while participants are reading the handout, pretend to notice this mistake. Blow the whistle to get participants' attention and make an announcement similar to this:

> *I have noticed a mistake in your handout. Let's get it corrected.*
>
> *Please locate the paragraph with the heading "Winning Tricks." The second sentence reads*
>
> *"The person who played this card gathers up the trick and places it face in front of him or her."*
>
> *This is incorrect. It should read:*
>
> *"The person who played this card gathers up the trick and places it face* down *in front of him or her."*
>
> *Please make this correction now.*

This brief action subtly suggests to the participants that they all have identical sets of rules.

FIVE TRICKS

Cards   Only 24 cards are used—Ace, 2, 3, 4, 5, and 6 in each suit (hearts, diamonds, clubs, spades). Ace is the highest card.

Players   Four—two sets of partners seated opposite each other.

Deal   The tallest person is the first dealer. The dealer shuffles the cards and deals them one at a time until each player has five cards. The remaining four cards are not used in the game. They are placed aside, face down.

Start   The player to the left of the dealer starts by leading (playing) any card. Other players take turns playing a card. The four cards played constitute a trick.

Winning Tricks   When all four players have played a card, the highest card wins the trick. The person who played this card gathers up the trick and places it face in front of him or her.

Play   The winner of the trick plays the first card for the next round. This procedure is repeated until all cards have been played.

Following Suit   The first player for each round may play any suit. All other players must follow suit (which means they should play a card of the same suit). If you do not have a card of the first suit played, then you may play a card of any suit.

Trumps   In this game there are no trumps, so players must follow suit whenever possible. If you do not have a card of the first suit played, then you must play a card of any suit. You don't win the trick even if you played a high card because it is not of the same suit as the first card for that round.

Continuation   Game ends when all five tricks have been played. Record the number of tricks won by each partnership. Immediately begin the next game with a new dealer (the player seated to the left of the previous dealer).

Ending   When time is called, complete the trick you are currently playing. Do not play any more tricks. Add up the total number of tricks for each partnership to decide who won.

FIVE TRICKS

Cards
Only 24 cards are used—Ace, 2, 3, 4, 5, and 6 in each suit (hearts, diamonds, clubs, spades). Ace is the highest card.

Players
Four—two sets of partners seated opposite each other.

Deal
The tallest person is the first dealer. The dealer shuffles the cards and deals them one at a time until each player has five cards. The remaining four cards are not used in the game. They are placed aside, face down.

Start
The player to the left of the dealer starts by leading (playing) any card. Other players take turns playing a card. The four cards played constitute a trick.

Winning Tricks
When all four players have played a card, the highest card wins the trick. The person who played this card gathers up the trick and places it face in front of him or her.

Play
The winner of the trick plays the first card for the next round. This procedure is repeated until all cards have been played.

Following Suit
The first player for each round may play any suit. All other players must follow suit (which means they should play a card of the same suit). If you do not have a card of the first suit played, then you may play a card of any suit.

Trumps
In this game spades are trumps, which are only played if you cannot follow suit. You win the trick even if the spade you played is a low card, unless someone else plays a higher spade.

Continuation
Game ends when all five tricks have been played. Record the number of tricks won by each partnership. Immediately begin the next game with a new dealer (the player seated to the left of the previous dealer).

Ending
When time is called, complete the trick you are currently playing. Do not play any more tricks. Add up the total number of tricks for each partnership to decide who won.

FIVE TRICKS

Cards
Only 24 cards are used—Ace, 2, 3, 4, 5, and 6 in each suit (hearts, diamonds, clubs, spades). Ace is the lowest card.

Players
Four—two sets of partners seated opposite each other.

Deal
The tallest person is the first dealer. The dealer shuffles the cards and deals them one at a time until each player has five cards. The remaining four cards are not used in the game. They are placed aside, face down.

Start
The player to the left of the dealer starts by leading (playing) any card. Other players take turns playing a card. The four cards played constitute a trick.

Winning Tricks
When all four players have played a card, the highest card wins the trick. The person who played this card gathers up the trick and places it face in front of him or her.

Play
The winner of the trick plays the first card for the next round. This procedure is repeated until all cards have been played.

Following Suit
The first player for each round may play any suit. All other players must follow suit (which means they should play a card of the same suit). If you do not have a card of the first suit played, then you may play a card of any suit.

Trumps
In this game spades are trumps, which are only played if you cannot follow suit. You win the trick even if the spade you played is a low card, unless someone else plays a higher spade.

Continuation
Game ends when all five tricks have been played. Record the number of tricks won by each partnership. Immediately begin the next game with a new dealer (the player seated to the left of the previous dealer).

Ending
When time is called, complete the trick you are currently playing. Do not play any more tricks. Add up the total number of tricks for each partnership to decide who won.

FIVE TRICKS

Cards Only 24 cards are used—Ace, 2, 3, 4, 5, and 6 in each suit (hearts, diamonds, clubs, spades). Ace is the lowest card.

Players Four—two sets of partners seated opposite each other.

Deal The tallest person is the first dealer. The dealer shuffles the cards and deals them one at a time until each player has five cards. The remaining four cards are not used in the game. They are placed aside, face down.

Start The player to the left of the dealer starts by leading (playing) any card. Other players take turns playing a card. The four cards played constitute a trick.

Winning Tricks When all four players have played a card, the highest card wins the trick. The person who played this card gathers up the trick and places it face in front of him or her.

Play The winner of the trick plays the first card for the next round. This procedure is repeated until all cards have been played.

Following Suit The first player for each round may play any suit. All other players must follow suit (which means they should play a card of the same suit). If you do not have a card of the first suit played, then you may play a card of any suit.

Trumps In this game spades are trumps, which can be played at any time. (You don't have to follow suit if you decide to play a trump.) You win the trick even if the spade you played is a low card, unless someone else has played a higher spade.

Continuation Game ends when all five tricks have been played. Record the number of tricks won by each partnership. Immediately begin the next game with a new dealer (the player seated to the left of the previous dealer).

Ending When time is called, complete the trick you are currently playing. Do not play any more tricks. Add up the total number of tricks for each partnership to decide who won.

FIVE TRICKS

Cards Only 24 cards are used—Ace, 2, 3, 4, 5, and 6 in each suit (hearts, diamonds, clubs, spades). Ace is the highest card.

Players Four—two sets of partners seated opposite each other.

Deal The tallest person is the first dealer. The dealer shuffles the cards and deals them one at a time until each player has five cards. The remaining four cards are not used in the game. They are placed aside, face down.

Start The player to the left of the dealer starts by leading (playing) any card. Other players take turns playing a card. The four cards played constitute a trick.

Winning Tricks When all four players have played a card, the highest card wins the trick. The person who played this card gathers up the trick and places it face in front of him or her.

Play The winner of the trick plays the first card for the next round. This procedure is repeated until all cards have been played.

Following Suit The first player for each round may play any suit. All other players must follow suit (which means they should play a card of the same suit). If you do not have a card of the first suit played, then you may play a card of any suit.

Trumps In this game spades are trumps, which can be played at any time. (You don't have to follow suit if you decide to play a trump.) You win the trick even if the spade you played is a low card, unless someone else has played a higher spade.

Continuation Game ends when all five tricks have been played. Record the number of tricks won by each partnership. Immediately begin the next game with a new dealer (the player seated to the left of the previous dealer).

Ending When time is called, complete the trick you are currently playing. Do not play any more tricks. Add up the total number of tricks for each partnership to decide who won.

FIVE TRICKS

Cards Only 24 cards are used—Ace, 2, 3, 4, 5, and 6 in each suit (hearts, diamonds, clubs, spades). Ace is the highest card.

Players Four—two sets of partners seated opposite each other.

Deal The tallest person is the first dealer. The dealer shuffles the cards and deals them one at a time until each player has five cards. The remaining four cards are not used in the game. They are placed aside, face down.

Start The player to the left of the dealer starts by leading (playing) any card. Other players take turns playing a card. The four cards played constitute a trick.

Winning Tricks When all four players have played a card, the highest card wins the trick. The person who played this card gathers up the trick and places it face in front of him or her.

Play The winner of the trick plays the first card for the next round. This procedure is repeated until all cards have been played.

Following Suit The first player for each round may play any suit. All other players must follow suit (which means they should play a card of the same suit). If you do not have a card of the first suit played, then you may play a card of any suit.

Trumps In this game diamonds are trumps, which can be played at any time. (You don't have to follow suit if you decide to play a trump.) You win the trick even if the diamond you played is a low card, unless someone else has played a higher diamond.

Continuation Game ends when all five tricks have been played. Record the number of tricks won by each partnership. Immediately begin the next game with a new dealer (the player seated to the left of the previous dealer).

Ending When time is called, complete the trick you are currently playing. Do not play any more tricks. Add up the total number of tricks for each partnership to decide who won.

FIVE TRICKS

Cards Only 24 cards are used—Ace, 2, 3, 4, 5, and 6 in each suit (hearts, diamonds, clubs, spades). Ace is the lowest card.

Players Four—two sets of partners seated opposite each other.

Deal The tallest person is the first dealer. The dealer shuffles the cards and deals them one at a time until each player has five cards. The remaining four cards are not used in the game. They are placed aside, face down.

Start The player to the left of the dealer starts by leading (playing) any card. Other players take turns playing a card. The four cards played constitute a trick.

Winning Tricks When all four players have played a card, the highest card wins the trick. The person who played this card gathers up the trick and places it face in front of him or her.

Play The winner of the trick plays the first card for the next round. This procedure is repeated until all cards have been played.

Following Suit The first player for each round may play any suit. All other players must follow suit (which means they should play a card of the same suit). If you do not have a card of the first suit played, then you may play a card of any suit.

Trumps In this game diamonds are trumps, which can be played at any time. (You don't have to follow suit if you decide to play a trump.) You win the trick even if the diamond you played is a low card, unless someone else has played a higher diamond.

Continuation Game ends when all five tricks have been played. Record the number of tricks won by each partnership. Immediately begin the next game with a new dealer (the player seated to the left of the previous dealer).

Ending When time is called, complete the trick you are currently playing. Do not play any more tricks. Add up the total number of tricks for each partnership to decide who won.

FIVE TRICKS

Cards	Only 24 cards are used—Ace, 2, 3, 4, 5, and 6 in each suit (hearts, diamonds, clubs, spades). Ace is the lowest card.
Players	Four—two sets of partners seated opposite each other.
Deal	The tallest person is the first dealer. The dealer shuffles the cards and deals them one at a time until each player has five cards. The remaining four cards are not used in the game. They are placed aside, face down.
Start	The player to the left of the dealer starts by leading (playing) any card. Other players take turns playing a card. The four cards played constitute a trick.
Winning Tricks	When all four players have played a card, the highest card wins the trick. The person who played this card gathers up the trick and places it face in front of him or her.
Play	The winner of the trick plays the first card for the next round. This procedure is repeated until all cards have been played.
Following Suit	The first player for each round may play any suit. All other players must follow suit (which means they should play a card of the same suit). If you do not have a card of the first suit played, then you may play a card of any suit.
Trumps	In this game diamonds are trumps, which are only played if you cannot follow suit. You win the trick even if the diamond you played is a low card, unless someone else plays a higher diamond.
Continuation	Game ends when all five tricks have been played. Record the number of tricks won by each partnership. Immediately begin the next game with a new dealer (the player seated to the left of the previous dealer).
Ending	When time is called, complete the trick you are currently playing. Do not play any more tricks. Add up the total number of tricks for each partnership to decide who won.

FIVE TRICKS

Cards Only 24 cards are used—Ace, 2, 3, 4, 5, and 6 in each suit (hearts, diamonds, clubs, spades). Ace is the highest card.

Players Four—two sets of partners seated opposite each other.

Deal The tallest person is the first dealer. The dealer shuffles the cards and deals them one at a time until each player has five cards. The remaining four cards are not used in the game. They are placed aside, face down.

Start The player to the left of the dealer starts by leading (playing) any card. Other players take turns playing a card. The four cards played constitute a trick.

Winning Tricks When all four players have played a card, the highest card wins the trick. The person who played this card gathers up the trick and places it face in front of him or her.

Play The winner of the trick plays the first card for the next round. This procedure is repeated until all cards have been played.

Following Suit The first player for each round may play any suit. All other players must follow suit (which means they should play a card of the same suit). If you do not have a card of the first suit played, then you may play a card of any suit.

Trumps In this game diamonds are trumps, which are only played if you cannot follow suit. You win the trick even if the diamond you played is a low card, unless someone else plays a higher diamond.

Continuation Game ends when all five tricks have been played. Record the number of tricks won by each partnership. Immediately begin the next game with a new dealer (the player seated to the left of the previous dealer).

Ending When time is called, complete the trick you are currently playing. Do not play any more tricks. Add up the total number of tricks for each partnership to decide who won.

FIVE TRICKS

Cards   Only 24 cards are used—Ace, 2, 3, 4, 5, and 6 in each suit (hearts, diamonds, clubs, spades). Ace is the lowest card.

Players   Four—two sets of partners seated opposite each other.

Deal   The tallest person is the first dealer. The dealer shuffles the cards and deals them one at a time until each player has five cards. The remaining four cards are not used in the game. They are placed aside, face down.

Start   The player to the left of the dealer starts by leading (playing) any card. Other players take turns playing a card. The four cards played constitute a trick.

Winning Tricks   When all four players have played a card, the highest card wins the trick. The person who played this card gathers up the trick and places it face in front of him or her.

Play   The winner of the trick plays the first card for the next round. This procedure is repeated until all cards have been played.

Following Suit   The first player for each round may play any suit. All other players must follow suit (which means they should play a card of the same suit). If you do not have a card of the first suit played, then you may play a card of any suit.

Trumps   In this game there are no trumps, so players must follow suit whenever possible. If you do not have a card of the first suit played, then you must play a card of any suit. You don't win the trick even if you played a high card because it is not of the same suit as the first card for that round.

Continuation Game ends when all five tricks have been played. Record the number of tricks won by each partnership. Immediately begin the next game with a new dealer (the player seated to the left of the previous dealer).

Ending   When time is called, complete the trick you are currently playing. Do not play any more tricks. Add up the total number of tricks for each partnership to decide who won.

FIVE TRICKS for Three Players

Cards
Only 16 cards used. They are A, 2, 3, and 4 in each suit. Ace is the lowest card in each suit.

Players
Three. Each player plays for himself or herself.

Deal
The tallest person is selected to be the first dealer. The dealer shuffles the cards and deals them one at a time until each player has five cards. The remaining card is placed aside, face down. This card is not used in this round of the game.

Start
The player to the left of the dealer starts by leading (playing) any card. Other players take turns playing a card. The three cards played constitute a trick.

Winning Tricks
When all three players have played a card, the highest card wins the trick. The person who played this card gathers up the trick and places it face in front of him or her.

Play
The winner of the trick plays the first card for the next round. The procedure is repeated until all cards have been played.

Following Suit
The first player for each round may play a card of any suit. All other players must follow suit (which means that they should play a card of the same suit).

Discarding
If you don't have a card of the first suit, play a card of any other suit. The trick is won by the highest card of the original suit.

Continuation
Game ends when all five tricks have been played. Record the number of tricks won by each player. Immediately begin the next game with a new dealer (the player seated to the left of the previous dealer).

Conclusion
When time is called, complete the trick you are currently playing. Do not play any more tricks. Record the number of tricks that you currently have. Add up the total number of tricks for each player to decide who won.

FIVE TRICKS for Three Players

Cards

Only 16 cards used. They are A, 2, 3, and 4 in each suit. Ace is the highest card in each suit.

Players

Three. Each player plays for himself or herself.

Deal

The tallest person is selected to be the first dealer. The dealer shuffles the cards and deals them one at a time until each player has five cards. The remaining card is placed aside, face down. This card is not used in this round of the game.

Start

The player to the left of the dealer starts by leading (playing) any card. Other players take turns playing a card. The three cards played constitute a trick.

Winning Tricks

When all three players have played a card, the highest card wins the trick. The person who played this card gathers up the trick and places it face in front of him or her.

Play

The winner of the trick plays the first card for the next round. The procedure is repeated until all cards have been played.

Following Suit

The first player for each round may play a card of any suit. All other players must follow suit (which means that they should play a card of the same suit).

Discarding

If you don't have a card of the first suit, play a card of any other suit. The trick is won by the highest card of the original suit.

Continuation

Game ends when all five tricks have been played. Record the number of tricks won by each player. Immediately begin the next game with a new dealer (the player seated to the left of the previous dealer).

Conclusion

When time is called, complete the trick you are currently playing. Do not play any more tricks. Record the number of tricks that you currently have. Add up the total number of tricks for each player to decide who won.

French

Explorer . . .

- L'pprentissage coopératif
- Le jeu compétitif

Consignes

- Former des groupes de quatre
- S'asseoir autour d'une table

Apprendre
CINQ PLIS

- Lire la feuille distribuée
- Choisir un partenaire

Décret de bâillon

- NON: Paroles
- OUI: Gestes
- NON: Mots écrits
- OUI: Dessins

Tournois

- Jouer CINQ PLIS
- Jouer pendant 5 minutes
- Jouer plusieurs tours
- Noter le score

Règles de CINQ PLIS ("Five Tricks")

Traduit de l'anglais par Nancy Bragard

Dans toutes les versions des règles, nous avons volontairement omis un mot dans le paragraphe qui commence par "Gagner les plis".

En tout début du jeu, alors que les participants sont en train de lire les consignes, faites semblant de remarquer cette erreur. Marquez un temps d'arrêt, assurez-vous d'avoir l'attention des participants et faites une annonce semblable à celle-ci:

> *Je viens de remarquer une erreur dans vos consignes. Corrigeons-la.*
> *Trouvez le paragraphe qui commence "Gagner les plis". La deuxième*
> *phrase, "Celui qui a joué cette carte le pli et le place, retourné, devant lui"*
> *Est mal écrite. Elle devrait être:*
> *"Celui qui a joué cette carte ramasse le pli et le place, retourné, devant lui."*
> *Tenez compte de cette correction.*

Cette petite modification suggère de manière subtile aux participants qu'ils ont tous les mêmes règles.

CINQ PLIS

Cartes On joue avec seulement 24 cartes—Ace, 2, 3, 4, 5, et 6 dans chaque couleur (cœurs, carreaux, trèfles, piques). L'ace est la carte la plus forte.

Joueurs Quatre—deux équipes, les partenaires assis l'un en face de l'autre.

Distribution Le joueur le plus grand est le premier à distribuer. Celui-ci brasse les cartes et les distribue une à une jusqu'à ce que chaque joueur ait cinq cartes. Les quatre cartes restantes ne sont pas utilisées dans le jeu. Elles sont mises à l'écart, retournées.

Début Le joueur à gauche du distributeur commence en ouvrant avec n'importe quelle carte. Les autres joueurs jouent à tour de rôle. Les quatre cartes jouées constituent un pli.

Gagner les plis Quand les quatre joueurs auront joué, la carte la plus forte remporte le pli. Celui qui a joué cette carte ramasse le pli et le place, retourné, devant lui.

Le jeu Celui qui a remporté le pli joue la première carte du tour suivant. On continue ainsi jusqu'à ce que toutes les carte soient jouées.

Suivre la couleur Celui qui ouvre le tour peut jouer n'importe quelle couleur. Tous les autres joueurs doivent suivre cette couleur (jouent une carte de la même couleur). Si vous n'avez pas de carte de cette couleur, vous pouvez jouer n'importe quelle couleur.

Atouts Il n'y a pas d'atouts dans ce jeu, les joueurs doivent donc suivre la couleur lorsqu'ils en ont en main. Si vous n'avez pas la couleur de la carte jouée à l'ouverture du tour, vous devez jouer une carte d'une autre couleur. Vous ne gagnez pas le pli si vous jouez une autre couleur que celle qui est demandée, même si votre carte est plus forte.

Continuation Le jeu est fini quand les cinq plis sont joués. Notez le nombre de plis gagnés par chaque équipe. Commencez aussitôt une autre partie avec un nouveau distributeur, le joueur qui est à gauche du distributeur précédent.

Fin de jeu Lorsque l'animateur indique la fin du jeu, finissez le pli que vous êtes en train de jouer. Ne lancez pas d'autres tours. Comptez tous les plis gagnés par les deux équipes pour déterminer l'équipe vainqueur.

CINQ PLIS

Cartes On joue avec seulement 24 cartes—Ace, 2, 3, 4, 5, et 6 dans chaque couleur (cœurs, carreaux, trèfles, piques). L'ace est la carte la plus forte.

Joueurs Quatre—deux équipes, les partenaires assis l'un en face de l'autre.

Distribution Le joueur le plus grand est le premier à distribuer. Celui-ci brasse les cartes et les distribue une à une jusqu'à ce que chaque joueur ait cinq cartes. Les quatre cartes restantes ne sont pas utilisées dans le jeu. Elles sont mises à l'écart, retournées.

Début Le joueur à gauche du distributeur commence en ouvrant avec n'importe quelle carte. Les autres joueurs jouent à tour de rôle. Les quatre cartes jouées constituent un pli.

Gagner les plis Quand les quatre joueurs auront joué, la carte la plus forte remporte le pli. Celui qui a joué cette carte ramasse le pli et le place, retourné, devant lui.

Le jeu Celui qui a remporté le pli joue la première carte du tour suivant. On continue ainsi jusqu'à ce que toutes les carte soient jouées.

Suivre la couleur Celui qui ouvre le tour peut jouer n'importe quelle couleur. Tous les autres joueurs doivent suivre cette couleur (jouent une carte de la même couleur). Si vous n'avez pas de carte de cette couleur, vous pouvez jouer n'importe quelle couleur.

Atouts Dans ce jeu l'atout est pique. Vous ne pouvez jouer atout que si vous n'avez pas la couleur demandée. L'atout le plus fort joué emporte le pli.

Continuation Le jeu est fini quand les cinq plis sont joués. Notez le nombre de plis gagnés par chaque équipe. Commencez aussitôt une autre partie avec un nouveau distributeur, le joueur qui est à gauche du distributeur précédent.

Fin de jeu Lorsque l'animateur indique la fin du jeu, finissez le pli que vous êtes en train de jouer. Ne lancez pas d'autres tours. Comptez tous les plis gagnés par les deux équipes pour déterminer l'équipe vainqueur.

CINQ PLIS

Cartes

On joue avec seulement 24 cartes—Ace, 2, 3, 4, 5, et 6 dans chaque couleur (cœurs, carreaux, trèfles, piques). L'ace est la carte la plus faible.

Joueurs

Quatre—deu équipes, les partenaires assis l'un en face de l'autre.

Distribution

Le joueur le plus grand est le premier à distribuer. Celui-ci brasse les cartes et les distribue une à une jusqu'à ce que chaque joueur ait cinq cartes. Les quatre cartes restantes ne sont pas utilisées dans le jeu. Elles sont mises à l'écart, retournées.

Début

Le joueur à gauche du distributeur commence en ouvrant avec n'importe quelle carte. Les autres joueurs jouent à tour de rôle. Les quatre cartes jouées constituent un pli.

Gagner les plis

Quand les quatre joueurs auront joué, la carte la plus forte remporte le pli. Celui qui a joué cette carte ramasse le pli et le place, retourné, devant lui.

Le jeu

Celui qui a remporté le pli joue la première carte du tour suivant. On continue ainsi jusqu'à ce que toutes les carte soient jouées.

Suivre la couleur

Celui qui ouvre le tour peut jouer n'importe quelle couleur. Tous les autres joueurs doivent suivre cette couleur (jouent une carte de la même couleur). Si vous n'avez pas de carte de cette couleur, vous pouvez jouer n'importe quelle couleur.

Atouts

Dans ce jeu l'atout est pique. Vous ne pouvez jouer atout que si vous n'avez pas la couleur demandée. L'atout le plus fort joué emporte le pli.

Continuation

Le jeu est fini quand les cinq plis sont joués. Notez le nombre de plis gagnés par chaque équipe. Commencez aussitôt une autre partie avec un nouveau distributeur, le joueur qui est à gauche du distributeur précédent.

Fin de jeu

Lorsque l'animateur indique la fin du jeu, finissez le pli que vous êtes en train de jouer. Ne lancez pas d'autres tours. Comptez tous les plis gagnés par les deux équipes pour déterminer l'équipe vainqueur.

CINQ PLIS

Cartes On joue avec seulement 24 cartes—Ace, 2, 3, 4, 5, et 6 dans chaque couleur (cœurs, carreaux, trèfles, piques). L'ace est la carte la plus faible.

Joueurs Quatre—deux équipes, les partenaires assis l'un en face de l'autre.

Distribution Le joueur le plus grand est le premier à distribuer. Celui-ci brasse les cartes et les distribue une à une jusqu'à ce que chaque joueur ait cinq cartes. Les quatre cartes restantes ne sont pas utilisées dans le jeu. Elles sont mises à l'écart, retournées.

Début Le joueur à gauche du distributeur commence en ouvrant avec n'importe quelle carte. Les autres joueurs jouent à tour de rôle. Les quatre cartes jouées constituent un pli.

Gagner les plis Quand les quatre joueurs auront joué, la carte la plus forte remporte le pli. Celui qui a joué cette carte ramasse le pli et le place, retourné, devant lui.

Le jeu Celui qui a remporté le pli joue la première carte du tour suivant. On continue ainsi jusqu'à ce que toutes les carte soient jouées.

Suivre la couleur Celui qui ouvre le tour peut jouer n'importe quelle couleur. Tous les autres joueurs doivent suivre cette couleur (jouent une carte de la même couleur). Si vous n'avez pas de carte de cette couleur, vous pouvez jouer n'importe quelle couleur.

Atouts Dans ce jeu l'atout est pique. Vous pouvez jouer atout quand vous voulez (vous n'êtes pas obligé de suivre la couleur demandée). L'atout le plus fort joué emporte le pli.

Continuation Le jeu est fini quand les cinq plis sont joués. Notez le nombre de plis gagnés par chaque équipe. Commencez aussitôt une autre partie avec un nouveau distributeur, le joueur qui est à gauche du distributeur précédent.

Fin de jeu Lorsque l'animateur indique la fin du jeu, finissez le pli que vous êtes en train de jouer. Ne lancez pas d'autres tours. Comptez tous les plis gagnés par les deux équipes pour déterminer l'équipe vainqueur.

CINQ PLIS

Cartes   On joue avec seulement 24 cartes—Ace, 2, 3, 4, 5, et 6 dans chaque couleur (cœurs, carreaux, trèfles, piques). L'ace est la carte la plus forte.

Joueurs   Quatre—deux équipes, les partenaires assis l'un en face de l'autre.

Distribution   Le joueur le plus grand est le premier à distribuer. Celui-ci brasse les cartes et les distribue une à une jusqu'à ce que chaque joueur ait cinq cartes. Les quatre cartes restantes ne sont pas utilisées dans le jeu. Elles sont mises à l'écart, retournées.

Début   Le joueur à gauche du distributeur commence en ouvrant avec n'importe quelle carte. Les autres joueurs jouent à tour de rôle. Les quatre cartes jouées constituent un pli.

Gagner les plis   Quand les quatre joueurs auront joué, la carte la plus forte remporte le pli. Celui qui a joué cette carte ramasse le pli et le place, retourné, devant lui.

Le jeu   Celui qui a remporté le pli joue la première carte du tour suivant. On continue ainsi jusqu'à ce que toutes les carte soient jouées.

Suivre la couleur   Celui qui ouvre le tour peut jouer n'importe quelle couleur. Tous les autres joueurs doivent suivre cette couleur (jouent une carte de la même couleur). Si vous n'avez pas de carte de cette couleur, vous pouvez jouer n'importe quelle couleur.

Atouts   Dans ce jeu l'atout est pique. Vous pouvez jouer atout quand vous voulez (vous n'êtes pas obligé de suivre la couleur demandée). L'atout le plus fort joué emporte le pli.

Continuation   Le jeu est fini quand les cinq plis sont joués. Notez le nombre de plis gagnés par chaque équipe. Commencez aussitôt une autre partie avec un nouveau distributeur, le joueur qui est à gauche du distributeur précédent.

Fin de jeu   Lorsque l'animateur indique la fin du jeu, finissez le pli que vous êtes en train de jouer. Ne lancez pas d'autres tours. Comptez tous les plis gagnés par les deux équipes pour déterminer l'équipe vainqueur.

CINQ PLIS

Cartes   On joue avec seulement 24 cartes—Ace, 2, 3, 4, 5, et 6 dans chaque couleur (cœurs, carreaux, trèfles, piques). L'ace est la carte la plus forte.

Joueurs   Quatre—deux équipes, les partenaires assis l'un en face de l'autre.

Distribution   Le joueur le plus grand est le premier à distribuer. Celui-ci brasse les cartes et les distribue une à une jusqu'à ce que chaque joueur ait cinq cartes. Les quatre cartes restantes ne sont pas utilisées dans le jeu. Elles sont mises à l'écart, retournées.

Début   Le joueur à gauche du distributeur commence en ouvrant avec n'importe quelle carte. Les autres joueurs jouent à tour de rôle. Les quatre cartes jouées constituent un pli.

Gagner les plis   Quand les quatre joueurs auront joué, la carte la plus forte remporte le pli. Celui qui a joué cette carte ramasse le pli et le place, retourné, devant lui.

Le jeu   Celui qui a remporté le pli joue la première carte du tour suivant. On continue ainsi jusqu'à ce que toutes les carte soient jouées.

Suivre la couleur   Celui qui ouvre le tour peut jouer n'importe quelle couleur. Tous les autres joueurs doivent suivre cette couleur (jouent une carte de la même couleur). Si vous n'avez pas de carte de cette couleur, vous pouvez jouer n'importe quelle couleur.

Atouts   Dans ce jeu l'atout est carreau. Vous pouvez jouer atout quand vous voulez (vous n'êtes pas obligé de suivre la couleur demandée). L'atout le plus fort joué emporte le pli.

Continuation   Le jeu est fini quand les cinq plis sont joués. Notez le nombre de plis gagnés par chaque équipe. Commencez aussitôt une autre partie avec un nouveau distributeur, le joueur qui est à gauche du distributeur précédent.

Fin de jeu   Lorsque l'animateur indique la fin du jeu, finissez le pli que vous êtes en train de jouer. Ne lancez pas d'autres tours. Comptez tous les plis gagnés par les deux équipes pour déterminer l'équipe vainqueur.

CINQ PLIS

Cartes On joue avec seulement 24 cartes—Ace, 2, 3, 4, 5, et 6 dans chaque couleur (cœurs, carreaux, trèfles, piques). L'ace est la carte la plus faible.

Joueurs Quatre—deux équipes, les partenaires assis l'un en face de l'autre.

Distribution Le joueur le plus grand est le premier à distribuer. Celui-ci brasse les cartes et les distribue une à une jusqu'à ce que chaque joueur a cinq cartes. Les quatre cartes restantes ne sont pas utilisées dans le jeu. Elles sont mises à l'écart, retournées.

Début Le joueur à gauche du distributeur commence en ouvrant avec n'importe quelle carte. Les autres joueurs jouent à tour de rôle. Les quatre cartes jouées constituent un pli.

Gagner les plis Quand les quatre joueurs auront joué, la carte la plus forte remporte le pli. Celui qui a joué cette carte ramasse le pli et le place, retourné, devant lui.

Le jeu Celui qui a remporté le pli joue la première carte du tour suivant. On continue ainsi jusqu'à ce que toutes les carte soient jouées.

Suivre la couleur Celui qui ouvre le tour peut jouer n'importe quelle couleur. Tous les autres joueurs doivent suivre cette couleur (jouent une carte de la même couleur). Si vous n'avez pas de carte de cette couleur, vous pouvez jouer n'importe quelle couleur.

Atouts Dans ce jeu l'atout est carreau. Vous pouvez jouer atout quand vous voulez (vous n'êtes pas obligé de suivre la couleur demandée). L'atout le plus fort joué emporte le pli.

Continuation Le jeu est fini quand les cinq plis sont joués. Notez le nombre de plis gagnés par chaque équipe. Commencez aussitôt une autre partie avec un nouveau distributeur, le joueur qui est à gauche du distributeur précédent.

Fin de jeu Lorsque l'animateur indique la fin du jeu, finissez le pli que vous êtes en train de jouer. Ne lancez pas d'autres tours. Comptez tous les plis gagnés par les deux équipes pour déterminer l'équipe vainqueur.

CINQ PLIS

Cartes On joue avec seulement 24 cartes—Ace, 2, 3, 4, 5, et 6 dans chaque couleur (cœurs, carreaux, trèfles, piques). L'ace est la carte la plus faible.

Joueurs Quatre—deux équipes, les partenaires assis l'un en face de l'autre.

Distribution Le joueur le plus grand est le premier à distribuer. Celui-ci brasse les cartes et les distribue une à une jusqu'à ce que chaque joueur ait cinq cartes. Les quatre cartes restantes ne sont pas utilisées dans le jeu. Elles sont mises à l'écart, retournées.

Début Le joueur à gauche du distributeur commence en ouvrant avec n'importe quelle carte. Les autres joueurs jouent à tour de rôle. Les quatre cartes jouées constituent un pli.

Gagner les plis Quand les quatre joueurs auront joué, la carte la plus forte remporte le pli. Celui qui a joué cette carte ramasse le pli et le place, retourné, devant lui.

Le jeu Celui qui a remporté le pli joue la première carte du tour suivant. On continue ainsi jusqu'à ce que toutes les carte soient jouées.

Suivre la couleur Celui qui ouvre le tour peut jouer n'importe quelle couleur. Tous les autres joueurs doivent suivre cette couleur (jouent une carte de la même couleur). Si vous n'avez pas de carte de cette couleur, vous pouvez jouer n'importe quelle couleur.

Atouts Dans ce jeu l'atout est carreau. Vous ne pouvez jouer atout que si vous n'avez pas la couleur demandée. L'atout le plus fort joué emporte le pli.

Continuation Le jeu est fini quand les cinq plis sont joués. Notez le nombre de plis gagnés par chaque équipe. Commencez aussitôt une autre partie avec un nouveau distributeur, le joueur qui est à gauche du distributeur précédent.

Fin de jeu Lorsque l'animateur indique la fin du jeu, finissez le pli que vous êtes en train de jouer. Ne lancez pas d'autres tours. Comptez tous les plis gagnés par les deux équipes pour déterminer l'équipe vainqueur.

CINQ PLIS

Cartes
On joue avec seulement 24 cartes—Ace, 2, 3, 4, 5, et 6 dans chaque couleur (cœurs, carreaux, trèfles, piques). L'ace est la carte la plus forte.

Joueurs
Quatre—deux équipes, les partenaires assis l'un en face de l'autre.

Distribution
Le joueur le plus grand est le premier à distribuer. Celui-ci brasse les cartes et les distribue une à une jusqu'à ce que chaque joueur ait cinq cartes. Les quatre cartes restantes ne sont pas utilisées dans le jeu. Elles sont mises à l'écart, retournées.

Début
Le joueur à gauche du distributeur commence en ouvrant avec n'importe quelle carte. Les autres joueurs jouent à tour de rôle. Les quatre cartes jouées constituent un pli.

Gagner les plis
Quand les quatre joueurs auront joué, la carte la plus forte remporte le pli. Celui qui a joué cette carte ramasse le pli et le place, retourné, devant lui.

Le jeu
Celui qui a remporté le pli joue la première carte du tour suivant. On continue ainsi jusqu'à ce que toutes les carte soient jouées.

Suivre la couleur
Celui qui ouvre le tour peut jouer n'importe quelle couleur. Tous les autres joueurs doivent suivre cette couleur (jouent une carte de la même couleur). Si vous n'avez pas de carte de cette couleur, vous pouvez jouer n'importe quelle couleur.

Atouts
Dans ce jeu l'atout est carreau. Vous ne pouvez jouer atout que si vous n'avez pas la couleur demandée. L'atout le plus fort joué emporte le pli.

Continuation
Le jeu est fini quand les cinq plis sont joués. Notez le nombre de plis gagnés par chaque équipe. Commencez aussitôt une autre partie avec un nouveau distributeur, le joueur qui est à gauche du distributeur précédent.

Fin de jeu
Lorsque l'animateur indique la fin du jeu, finissez le pli que vous êtes en train de jouer. Ne lancez pas d'autres tours. Comptez tous les plis gagnés par les deux équipes pour déterminer l'équipe vainqueur.

CINQ PLIS

Cartes
On joue avec seulement 24 cartes—Ace, 2, 3, 4, 5, et 6 dans chaque couleur (cœurs, carreaux, trèfles, piques). L'ace est la carte la plus faible.

Joueurs
Quatre—deux équipes, les partenaires assis l'un en face de l'autre.

Distribution
Le joueur le plus grand est le premier à distribuer. Celui-ci brasse les cartes et les distribue une à une jusqu'à ce que chaque joueur ait cinq cartes. Les quatre cartes restantes ne sont pas utilisées dans le jeu. Elles sont mises à l'écart, retournées.

Début
Le joueur à gauche du distributeur commence en ouvrant avec n'importe quelle carte. Les autres joueurs jouent à tour de rôle. Les quatre cartes jouées constituent un pli.

Gagner les plis
Quand les quatre joueurs auront joué, la carte la plus forte remporte le pli. Celui qui a joué cette carte ramasse le pli et le place, retourné, devant lui.

Le jeu
Celui qui a remporté le pli joue la première carte du tour suivant. On continue ainsi jusqu'à ce que toutes les carte soient jouées.

Suivre la couleur
Celui qui ouvre le tour peut jouer n'importe quelle couleur. Tous les autres joueurs doivent suivre cette couleur (jouent une carte de la même couleur). Si vous n'avez pas de carte de cette couleur, vous pouvez jouer n'importe quelle couleur.

Atouts
Il n'y a pas d'atouts dans ce jeu, les joueurs doivent donc suivre la couleur lorsqu'ils en ont en main. Si vous n'avez pas la couleur de la carte jouée à l'ouverture du tour, vous devez jouer une carte d'une autre couleur. Vous ne gagnez pas le pli si vous jouez une autre couleur que celle qui est demandée, même si votre carte est plus forte.

Continuation
Le jeu est fini quand les cinq plis sont joués. Notez le nombre de plis gagnés par chaque équipe. Commencez aussitôt une autre partie avec un nouveau distributeur, le joueur qui est à gauche du distributeur précédent.

Fin de jeu
Lorsque l'animateur indique la fin du jeu, finissez le pli que vous êtes en train de jouer. Ne lancez pas d'autres tours. Comptez tous les plis gagnés par les deux équipes pour déterminer l'équipe vainqueur.

CINQ PLIS pour Trois Joueurs

Cartes On joue avec seulement 16 cartes—Ace, 2, 3, 4, dans chaque couleur (cœurs, carreaux, trèfles, piques). L'ace est la carte la plus *faible*.

Joueurs Trois, chaque joueur joue pour lui-même.

Distribution Le joueur le plus grand est le premier à distribuer. Celui-ci brasse les cartes et les distribue une à une jusqu'à ce que chaque joueur ait cinq cartes. La carte restante n'est pas utilisée dans ce tour du jeu.

Début Le joueur à gauche du distributeur commence en ouvrant avec n'importe quelle carte. Les autres joueurs jouent à tour de rôle. Les trois cartes jouées constituent un pli.

Gagner les plis Quand les trois joueurs auront joué, la carte la plus forte remporte le pli. Celui qui a joué cette carte ramasse le pli et le place, retourné, devant lui.

Le jeu Celui qui a remporté le pli joue la première carte du tour suivant. On continue ainsi jusqu'à ce que toutes les carte soient jouées.

Suivre la couleur Celui qui ouvre le tour peut jouer n'importe quelle couleur. Tous les autres joueurs doivent suivre la couleur demandée (jouent une carte de la même couleur).

Défausser Si vous n'avez pas de carte de la couleur demandée, jouez n'importe quelle carte. Le pli est emporté par la carte la plus forte de la *couleur demandée*.

Continuation Le jeu est fini quand les cinq plis sont joués. Notez le nombre de plis gagnés par chaque joueur. Commencez aussitôt une autre partie avec un nouveau distributeur, le joueur qui est à gauche du distributeur précédent.

Fin de jeu Lorsque l'animateur indique la fin du jeu, finissez le pli que vous êtes en train de jouer. Ne lancez pas d'autres tours. Contez les plis que vous avez gagné depuis le début du jeu, le joueur qui en a remporté le plus est le gagnant de votre table.

CINQ PLIS pour Trois Joueurs

Cartes   On joue avec seulement 16 cartes—Ace, 2, 3, 4, dans chaque couleur (cœurs, carreaux, trèfles, piques). L'ace est la carte la plus *forte*.

Joueurs   Trois, chaque joueur joue pour lui-même.

Distribution   Le joueur le plus grand est le premier à distribuer. Celui-ci brasse les cartes et les distribue une à une jusqu'à ce que chaque joueur ait cinq cartes. La carte restante n'est pas utilisée dans ce tour du jeu.

Début   Le joueur à gauche du distributeur commence en ouvrant avec n'importe quelle carte. Les autres joueurs jouent à tour de rôle. Les trois cartes jouées constituent un pli.

Gagner les plis   Quand les trois joueurs auront joué, la carte la plus forte remporte le pli. Celui qui a joué cette carte ramasse le pli et le place, retourné, devant lui.

Le jeu   Celui qui a remporté le pli joue la première carte du tour suivant. On continue ainsi jusqu'à ce que toutes les carte soient jouées.

Suivre la couleur   Celui qui ouvre le tour peut jouer n'importe quelle couleur. Tous les autres joueurs doivent suivre la couleur demandée (jouent une carte de la même couleur).

Défausser   Si vous n'avez pas de carte de la couleur demandée, jouez n'importe quelle carte. Le pli est emporté par la carte la plus forte de la *couleur demandée*.

Continuation   Le jeu est fini quand les cinq plis sont joués. Notez le nombre de plis gagnés par chaque joueur. Commencez aussitôt une autre partie avec un nouveau distributeur, le joueur qui est à gauche du distributeur précédent.

Fin de jeu   Lorsque l'animateur indique la fin du jeu, finissez le pli que vous êtes en train de jouer. Ne lancez pas d'autres tours. Contez les plis que vous avez gagné depuis le début du jeu, le joueur qui en a remporté le plus est le gagnant de votre table.

German

Was es zu
entdecken gibt . . . .

- Kooperatives Lernen
- Konkurrierendes Spielen

Anweisungen

- Bilden Sie Vierergruppen

- Setzen Sie sich gruppenweise um einen Tisch

Lernen Sie "Fünf Stiche"

- Lesen Sie das Regelblatt
- Wählen Sie Ihren Partner

Mundstillhalte-Regel

- Sprechen verboten
- Gesten erlaubt
- Schreiben verboten
- Zeichnen erlaubt

Tournier

- Spielen Sie "Fünf Stiche"
- Spielen Sie fünf Minuten lang
- Sielen Sie mehrere Runden
- Notieren Sie die Punkte

Regeln für Fünf Stiche ("Five Tricks")

Übersetzung von Samuel van den Bergh

Beachten Sie bitte:

In allen Versionen der Regeln haben wir absichtlich ein Wort weggelassen, und zwar im Abschnitt "Gewinn des Stichs (Stechen)".

Täuschen Sie vor, den Fehler zu bemerken, während die Spieler am Anfang des Spiels das Regelblatt lesen. Pfeifen Sie, um die Aufmerksamkeit der Teilnehmer zu erhaschen und erklären Sie zum Beispiel:

Ich habe einen Fehler in Ihrem Regelblatt entdeckt. Ich bitte Sie, ihn zu korrigieren.

Suchen Sie bitte den Abschnitt mit dem Titel "Gewinn des Stichs (Stechen)".

Der zweite Satz lautet:

„Wer diese gespielt hat, nimmt den Stich auf und legt ihn umgedreht vor."

Das kann so nicht stimmen. Es sollte heissen:

„Wer diese gespielt hat, nimmt den Stich auf und legt ihn umgedreht vor sich".

Bitte nehmen Sie diese Korrektur vor.

Dieses kleine Intermezzo verstärkt bei den Spielern den Glauben, dass sie alle die gleichen Regeln haben.

FÜNF STICHE

Karten
Es werden nur 24 Karten verwendet: Das Ass, die 2, die 3, die 4, die 5 und die 6 jeder Farbe (Herz, Karo, Kreuz, Pik). Das Ass ist die höchste Karte.

Spieler
Vier. Die zwei zusammengehörenden Paare sitzen sich gegenüber.

Verteilen
Die grösste Person verteilt zuerst. Sie mischt die Karten und verteilt eine nach der andern, bis jeder Spieler fünf Karten hat. Die verbleibenden vier Karten werden nicht verwendet und umgedreht beiseite gelegt.

Start
Der Spieler links vom Kartengeber beginnt und spielt eine beliebige Karte aus. Die andern spielen der Reihe nach eine Karte. Sind vier Karten gespielt, so stellen sie einen Stich dar.

Gewinn des Stichs (Stechen)
Wenn alle vier Mitspielenden eine Karte gespielt haben, so gewinnt die höchste Karte den Stich. Wer diese gespielt hat, nimmt den Stich auf und legt ihn umgedreht vor sich.

Spiel
Der Gewinner des Stichs spielt die erste Karte der nächsten Runde. Dieses Vorgehen wiederholt sich, bis alle Karten gespielt sind.

Farbe angeben
Der erste Spieler jeder Runde kann eine beliebige Farbe ausspielen. Die andern müssen Farbe angeben (das heisst, sie müssen eine Karte derselben Farbe spielen). Ist dies nicht möglich, so kann man eine beliebige andere Karte spielen.

Trumpf
In diesem Spiel gibt es keinen Trumpf, die Spieler müssen also wenn möglich Farbe bedienen. Können sie dies nicht, so müssen sie eine Karte einer andern Farbe spielen. Auch eine hohe Karte gewinnt den Stich nicht, wenn sie nicht von derselben Farbe ist wie die erste Karte der Runde.

Fortsetzung
Das Spiel endet, wenn alle fünf Stiche gespielt sind. Notieren Sie die Anzahl Stiche, die jedes Paar gewonnen hat. Beginnen Sie sofort das nächste Spiel mit einem neuen Kartengeber (der Spieler links des vorhergehenden Gebers).

Ende
Wenn die Zeit abgelaufen ist, so spielen Sie den Stich zu Ende, aber keine weiteren mehr. Zählen Sie die gewonnenen Stiche jedes Paars zusammen, um die Sieger zu ermitteln.

FÜNF STICHE

Karten	Es werden nur 24 Karten verwendet: Das Ass, die 2, die 3, die 4, die 5 und die 6 jeder Farbe (Herz, Karo, Kreuz, Pik). Das Ass ist die höchste Karte.
Spieler	Vier. Die zwei zusammengehörenden Paare sitzen sich gegenüber.
Verteilen	Die grösste Person verteilt zuerst. Sie mischt die Karten und verteilt eine nach der andern, bis jeder Spieler fünf Karten hat. Die verbleibenden vier Karten werden nicht verwendet und umgedreht beiseite gelegt.
Start	Der Spieler links vom Kartengeber beginnt und spielt eine beliebige Karte aus. Die andern spielen der Reihe nach eine Karte. Sind vier Karten gespielt, so stellen sie einen Stich dar.
Gewinn des Stichs (Stechen)	Wenn alle vier Mitspielenden eine Karte gespielt haben, so gewinnt die höchste Karte den Stich. Wer diese gespielt hat, nimmt den Stich auf und legt ihn umgedreht vor sich.
Spiel	Der Gewinner des Stichs spielt die erste Karte der nächsten Runde. Dieses Vorgehen wiederholt sich, bis alle Karten gespielt sind.
Farbe angeben	Der erste Spieler jeder Runde kann eine beliebige Farbe ausspielen. Die andern müssen Farbe angeben (das heisst, sie müssen eine Karte derselben Farbe spielen). Ist dies nicht möglich, so kann man eine beliebige andere Karte spielen.
Trumpf	In diesem Spiel ist Pik Trumpf. Pik wird nur gespielt, wenn man nicht Farbe bedienen kann. Auch eine tiefe Pik-Karte gewinnt den Stich, ausser jemand spielt eine höhere Pik-Karte.
Fortsetzung	Das Spiel endet, wenn alle fünf Stiche gespielt sind. Notieren Sie die Anzahl Stiche, die jedes Paar gewonnen hat. Beginnen Sie sofort das nächste Spiel mit einem neuen Kartengeber (der Spieler links des vorhergehenden Gebers).
Ende	Wenn die Zeit abgelaufen ist, so spielen Sie den Stich zu Ende, aber keine weiteren mehr. Zählen Sie die gewonnenen Stiche jedes Paars zusammen, um die Sieger zu ermitteln.

FÜNF STICHE

Karten Es werden nur 24 Karten verwendet: Das Ass, die 2, die 3, die 4, die 5 und die 6 jeder Farbe (Herz, Karo, Kreuz, Pik). Das Ass ist die tiefste Karte.

Spieler Vier. Die zwei zusammengehörenden Paare sitzen sich gegenüber.

Verteilen Die grösste Person verteilt zuerst. Sie mischt die Karten und verteilt eine nach der andern, bis jeder Spieler fünf Karten hat. Die verbleibenden vier Karten werden nicht verwendet und umgedreht beiseite gelegt.

Start Der Spieler links vom Kartengeber beginnt und spielt eine beliebige Karte aus. Die andern spielen der Reihe nach eine Karte. Sind vier Karten gespielt, so stellen sie einen Stich dar.

Gewinn des Stichs (Stechen) Wenn alle vier Mitspielenden eine Karte gespielt haben, so gewinnt die höchste Karte den Stich. Wer diese gespielt hat, nimmt den Stich auf und umgedreht vor sich.

Spiel Der Gewinner des Stichs spielt die erste Karte der nächsten Runde. Das Vorgehen wiederholt sich, bis alle Karten gespielt sind.

Farbe angeben Der erste Spieler jeder Runde kann eine beliebige Farbe ausspielen. Die andern müssen Farbe angeben (das heisst, sie müssen eine Karte derselben Farbe spielen). Ist dies nicht möglich, so kann man eine beliebige andere Karte spielen.

Trumpf In diesem Spiel ist Pik Trumpf. Pik wird nur gespielt, wenn man nicht Farbe bedienen kann. Auch eine tiefe Pik-Karte gewinnt den Stich, ausser jemand spielt eine höhere Pik-Karte.

Fortsetzung Das Spiel endet, wenn alle fünf Stiche gespielt sind. Notieren Sie die Anzahl Stiche, die jedes Paar gewonnen hat. Beginnen Sie sofort das nächste Spiel mit einem neuen Kartengeber (der Spieler links des vorhergehenden Gebers).

Ende Wenn die Zeit abgelaufen ist, so spielen Sie den Stich zu Ende, aber keine weiteren mehr. Zählen Sie die gewonnenen Stiche jedes Paars zusammen, um die Sieger zu ermitteln.

FÜNF STICHE

Karten Es werden nur 24 Karten verwendet: Das Ass, die 2, die 3, die 4, die 5 und die 6 jeder Farbe (Herz, Karo, Kreuz, Pik). Das Ass ist die tiefste Karte.

Spieler Vier. Die zwei zusammengehörenden Paare sitzen sich gegenüber.

Verteilen Die grösste Person verteilt zuerst. Sie mischt die Karten und verteilt eine nach der andern, bis jeder Spieler fünf Karten hat. Die verbleibenden vier Karten werden nicht verwendet und umgedreht beiseite gelegt.

Start Der Spieler links vom Kartengeber beginnt und spielt eine beliebige Karte aus. Die andern spielen der Reihe nach eine Karte. Sind vier Karten gespielt, so stellen sie einen Stich dar.

Gewinn des Stichs (Stechen) Wenn alle vier Mitspielenden eine Karte gespielt haben, so gewinnt die höchste Karte den Stich. Wer diese gespielt hat, nimmt den Stich auf und legt ihn umgedreht vor sich.

Spiel Der Gewinner des ersten Stichs spielt die erste Karte der nächsten Runde. Das Vorgehen wiederholt sich, bis alle Karten gespielt sind.

Farbe angeben Der erste Spieler jeder Runde kann eine beliebige Farbe ausspielen. Die andern müssen Farbe angeben (das heisst, sie müssen eine Karte derselben Farbe spielen). Ist dies nicht möglich, so kann man eine beliebige andere Karte spielen.

Trumpf In diesem Spiel ist Pik Trumpf. Pik kann jederzeit gespielt werden. (Man braucht nicht Farbe zu bedienen, wenn man einen Trumpf spielen will.) Eine tiefe Pik-Karte gewinnt den Stich, ausser jemand spielt eine höhere Pik-Karte.

Fortsetzung Das Spiel endet, wenn alle fünf Stiche gespielt sind. Notieren Sie die Anzahl Stiche, die jedes Paar gewonnen hat. Beginnen Sie sofort das nächste Spiel mit einem neuen Kartengeber (der Spieler links des ersten Gebers).

Ende Wenn die Zeit abgelaufen ist, so spielen Sie den Stich zu Ende, aber keine weiteren mehr. Zählen Sie die gewonnenen Stiche jedes Paars zusammen, um die Sieger zu ermitteln.

FÜNF STICHE

Karten	Es werden nur 24 Karten verwendet: Das Ass, die 2, die 3, die 4, die 5 und die 6 jeder Farbe (Herz, Karo, Kreuz, Pik). Das Ass ist die höchste Karte.
Spieler	Vier. Die zwei zusammengehörenden Paare sitzen sich gegenüber.
Verteilen	Die grösste Person verteilt zuerst. Sie mischt die Karten und verteilt eine nach der andern, bis jeder Spieler fünf Karten hat. Die verbleibenden vier Karten werden nicht verwendet und umgedreht beiseite gelegt.
Start	Der Spieler links vom Kartengeber beginnt und spielt eine beliebige Karte aus. Die andern spielen der Reihe nach eine Karte. Sind vier Karten gespielt, so stellen sie einen Stich dar.
Gewinn des Stichs (Stechen)	Wenn alle vier Mitspielenden eine Karte gespielt haben, so gewinnt die höchste Karte den Stich. Wer diese gespielt hat, nimmt den Stich auf und legt ihn umgedreht vor sich.
Spiel	Der Gewinner des ersten Stichs spielt die erste Karte der nächsten Runde. Das Vorgehen wiederholt sich, bis alle Karten gespielt sind.
Farbe angeben	Der erste Spieler jeder Runde kann eine beliebige Farbe ausspielen. Die andern müssen Farbe angeben (das heisst, sie müssen eine Karte derselben Farbe spielen). Ist dies nicht möglich, so kann man eine beliebige andere Karte spielen.
Trumpf	In diesem Spiel ist Pik Trumpf. Pik kann jederzeit gespielt werden. (Man braucht nicht Farbe zu bedienen, wenn man einen Trumpf spielen will.) Auch eine tiefe Pik-Karte gewinnt den Stich, ausser jemand spielt eine höhere Pik-Karte.
Fortsetzung	Das Spiel endet, wenn alle fünf Stiche gespielt sind. Notieren Sie die Anzahl Stiche, die jedes Paar gewonnen hat. Beginnen Sie sofort das nächste Spiel mit einem neuen Kartengeber (der Spieler links des ersten Gebers).
Ende	Wenn die Zeit abgelaufen ist, so spielen Sie den Stich zu Ende, aber keine weiteren mehr. Zählen Sie die gewonnenen Stiche jedes Paars zusammen, um die Sieger zu ermitteln.

FÜNF STICHE

Karten   Es werden nur 24 Karten verwendet: Das Ass, die 2, die 3, die 4, die 5 und die 6 jeder Farbe (Herz, Karo, Kreuz, Pik). Das Ass ist die höchste Karte.

Spieler   Vier. Die zwei zusammengehörenden Paare sitzen sich gegenüber.

Verteilen   Die grösste Person verteilt zuerst. Sie mischt die Karten und verteilt eine nach der andern, bis jeder Spieler fünf Karten hat. Die verbleibenden vier Karten werden nicht verwendet und umgedreht beiseite gelegt.

Start   Der Spieler links vom Kartengeber beginnt und spielt eine beliebige Karte aus. Die andern spielen der Reihe nach eine Karte. Sind vier Karten gespielt, so stellen sie einen Stich dar.

Gewinn des Stichs (Stechen)   Wenn alle vier Mitspielenden eine Karte gespielt haben, so gewinnt die höchste Karte den Stich. Wer diese gespielt hat, nimmt den Stich auf und legt ihn umgedreht vor sich.

Spiel   Der Gewinner des ersten Stichs spielt die erste Karte der nächsten Runde. Das Vorgehen wiederholt sich, bis alle Karten gespielt sind.

Farbe angeben   Der erste Spieler jeder Runde kann eine beliebige Farbe ausspielen. Die andern müssen Farbe angeben (das heisst, sie müssen eine Karte derselben Farbe spielen). Ist dies nicht möglich, so kann man eine beliebige andere Karte spielen.

Trumpf   In diesem Spiel ist Karo Trumpf. Karo kann jederzeit gespielt werden. (Man braucht nicht Farbe zu bedienen, wenn man einen Trumpf spielen will.) Auch eine tiefe Karo-Karte gewinnt den Stich, ausser jemand spielt eine höhere Karo-Karte.

Fortsetzung   Das Spiel endet, wenn alle fünf Stiche gespielt sind. Notieren Sie die Anzahl Stiche, die jedes Paar gewonnen hat. Beginnen Sie sofort das nächste Spiel mit einem neuen Kartengeber (der Spieler links des ersten Gebers).

Ende   Wenn die Zeit abgelaufen ist, so spielen Sie den Stich zu Ende, aber keine weiteren mehr. Zählen Sie die gewonnenen Stiche jedes Paars zusammen, um die Sieger zu ermitteln.

FÜNF STICHE

Karten
Es werden nur 24 Karten verwendet: Das Ass, die 2, die 3, die 4, die 5 und die 6 jeder Farbe (Herz, Karo, Kreuz, Pik). Das Ass ist die tiefste Karte.

Spieler
Vier. Die zwei zusammengehörenden Paare sitzen sich gegenüber.

Verteilen
Die grösste Person verteilt zuerst. Sie mischt die Karten und verteilt eine nach der andern, bis jeder Spieler fünf Karten hat. Die verbleibenden vier Karten werden nicht verwendet und umgedreht beiseite gelegt.

Start
Der Spieler links vom Kartengeber beginnt und spielt eine beliebige Karte aus. Die andern spielen der Reihe nach eine Karte. Sind vier Karten gespielt, so stellen sie einen Stich dar.

Gewinn des Stichs (Stechen)
Wenn alle vier Mitspielenden eine Karte gespielt haben, so gewinnt die höchste Karte den Stich. Wer diese gespielt hat, nimmt den Stich auf und legt ihn umgedreht vor sich.

Spiel
Der Gewinner des ersten Stichs spielt die erste Karte der nächsten Runde. Das Vorgehen wiederholt sich, bis alle Karten gespielt sind.

Farbe angeben
Der erste Spieler jeder Runde kann eine beliebige Farbe ausspielen. Die andern müssen Farbe angeben (das heisst, sie müssen eine Karte derselben Farbe spielen). Ist dies nicht möglich, so kann man eine beliebige andere Karte spielen.

Trumpf
In diesem Spiel ist Karo Trumpf. Karo kann jederzeit gespielt werden. (Man braucht nicht Farbe zu bedienen, wenn man einen Trumpf spielen will.) Auch eine tiefe Karo-Karte gewinnt den Stich, ausser jemand spielt eine höhere Karo-Karte.

Fortsetzung
Das Spiel endet, wenn alle fünf Stiche gespielt sind. Notieren Sie die Anzahl Stiche, die jedes Paar gewonnen hat. Beginnen Sie sofort das nächste Spiel mit einem neuen Kartengeber (der Spieler links des ersten Gebers).

Ende
Wenn die Zeit abgelaufen ist, so spielen Sie den Stich zu Ende, aber keine weiteren mehr. Zählen Sie die gewonnenen Stiche jedes Paars zusammen, um die Sieger zu ermitteln.

FÜNF STICHE

Karten
Es werden nur 24 Karten verwendet: Das Ass, die 2, die 3, die 4, die 5 und die 6 jeder Farbe (Herz, Karo, Kreuz, Pik). Das Ass ist die tiefste Karte.

Spieler
Vier. Die zwei zusammengehörenden Paare sitzen sich gegenüber.

Verteilen
Die grösste Person verteilt zuerst. Sie mischt die Karten und verteilt eine nach der andern, bis jeder Spieler fünf Karten hat. Die verbleibenden vier Karten werden nicht verwendet und umgedreht beiseite gelegt.

Start
Der Spieler links vom Kartengeber beginnt und spielt eine beliebige Karte aus. Die andern spielen der Reihe nach eine Karte. Sind vier Karten gespielt, so stellen sie einen Stich dar.

Gewinn des Stichs (Stechen)
Wenn alle vier Mitspielenden eine Karte gespielt haben, so gewinnt die höchste Karte den Stich. Wer diese gespielt hat, nimmt den Stich auf und legt ihn umgedreht vor sich.

Spiel
Der Gewinner des ersten Stichs spielt die erste Karte der nächsten Runde. Das Vorgehen wiederholt sich, bis alle Karten gespielt sind.

Farbe angeben
Der erste Spieler jeder Runde kann eine beliebige Farbe ausspielen. Die andern müssen Farbe angeben (das heisst, sie müssen eine Karte derselben Farbe spielen). Ist dies nicht möglich, so kann man eine beliebige andere Karte spielen.

Trumpf
In diesem Spiel ist Karo Trumpf. Karo wird nur gespielt, wenn man nicht Farbe bedienen kann. Auch eine tiefe Karo-Karte gewinnt den Stich, ausser jemand spielt eine höhere Karo-Karte.

Fortsetzung
Das Spiel endet, wenn alle fünf Stiche gespielt sind. Notieren Sie die Anzahl Stiche, die jedes Paar gewonnen hat. Beginnen Sie sofort das nächste Spiel mit einem neuen Kartengeber (der Spieler links des ersten Gebers).

Ende
Wenn die Zeit abgelaufen ist, so spielen Sie den Stich zu Ende, aber keine weiteren mehr. Zählen Sie die gewonnenen Stiche jedes Paars zusammen, um die Sieger zu ermitteln.

FÜNF STICHE

Karten Es werden nur 24 Karten verwendet: Das Ass, die 2, die 3, die 4, die 5 und die 6 jeder Farbe (Herz, Karo, Kreuz, Pik). Das Ass ist die höchste Karte.

Spieler Vier. Die zwei zusammengehörenden Paare sitzen sich gegenüber.

Verteilen Die grösste Person verteilt zuerst. Sie mischt die Karten und verteilt eine nach der andern, bis jeder Spieler fünf Karten hat. Die verbleibenden vier Karten werden nicht verwendet und umgedreht beiseite gelegt.

Start Der Spieler links vom Kartengeber beginnt und spielt eine beliebige Karte aus. Die andern spielen der Reihe nach eine Karte. Sind vier Karten gespielt, so stellen sie einen Stich dar.

Gewinn des Stichs (Stechen) Wenn alle vier Mitspielenden eine Karte gespielt haben, so gewinnt die höchste Karte den Stich. Wer diese gespielt hat, nimmt den Stich auf und legt ihn umgedreht vor sich.

Spiel Der Gewinner des ersten Stichs spielt die erste Karte der nächsten Runde. Das Vorgehen wiederholt sich, bis alle Karten gespielt sind.

Farbe angeben Der erste Spieler jeder Runde kann eine beliebige Farbe ausspielen. Die andern müssen Farbe angeben (das heisst, sie müssen eine Karte derselben Farbe spielen). Ist dies nicht möglich, so kann man eine beliebige andere Karte spielen.

Trumpf In diesem Spiel ist Karo Trumpf. Karo wird nur gespielt, wenn man nicht Farbe bedienen kann. Auch eine tiefe Karo-Karte gewinnt den Stich, ausser jemand spielt eine höhere Karo-Karte.

Fortsetzung Das Spiel endet, wenn alle fünf Stiche gespielt sind. Notieren Sie die Anzahl Stiche, die jedes Paar gewonnen hat. Beginnen Sie sofort das nächste Spiel mit einem neuen Kartengeber (der Spieler links des ersten Gebers).

Ende Wenn die Zeit abgelaufen ist, so spielen Sie den Stich zu Ende, aber keine weiteren mehr. Zählen Sie die gewonnenen Stiche jedes Paars zusammen, um die Sieger zu ermitteln.

FÜNF STICHE

Karten   Es werden nur 24 Karten verwendet: Das Ass, die 2, die 3, die 4, die 5 und die 6 jeder Farbe (Herz, Karo, Kreuz, Pik). Das Ass ist die tiefste Karte.

Spieler   Vier. Die zwei zusammengehörenden Paare sitzen sich gegenüber.

Verteilen   Die grösste Person verteilt zuerst. Sie mischt die Karten und verteilt eine nach der andern, bis jeder Spieler fünf Karten hat. Die verbleibenden vier Karten werden nicht verwendet und umgedreht beiseite gelegt.

Start   Der Spieler links vom Kartengeber beginnt und spielt eine beliebige Karte aus. Die andern spielen der Reihe nach eine Karte. Sind vier Karten gespielt, so stellen sie einen Stich dar.

Gewinn des Stichs (Stechen)   Wenn alle vier Mitspielenden eine Karte gespielt haben, so gewinnt die höchste Karte den Stich. Wer diese gespielt hat, nimmt den Stich auf und legt ihn umgedreht vor sich.

Spiel   Der Gewinner des ersten Stichs spielt die erste Karte der nächsten Runde. Das Vorgehen wiederholt sich, bis alle Karten gespielt sind.

Farbe angeben   Der erste Spieler jeder Runde kann eine beliebige Farbe ausspielen. Die andern müssen Farbe angeben (das heisst, sie müssen eine Karte derselben Farbe spielen). Ist dies nicht möglich, so kann man eine beliebige andere Karte spielen.

Trumpf   In diesem Spiel gibt es keinen Trumpf, die Spieler müssen also wenn möglich Farbe bedienen. Können sie dies nicht, so müssen sie eine Karte einer anderen Farbe spielen. Eine hohe Karte gewinnt den Stich nicht, wenn sie nicht von derselben Farbe ist wie die erste Karte der Runde.

Fortsetzung   Das Spiel endet, wenn alle fünf Stiche gespielt sind. Notieren Sie die Anzahl Stiche, die jedes Paar gewonnen hat. Beginnen Sie sofort das nächste Spiel mit einem neuen Kartengeber (der Spieler links des ersten Gebers).

Ende   Wenn die Zeit abgelaufen ist, so spielen Sie den Stich zu Ende, aber keine weiteren mehr. Zählen Sie die gewonnenen Stiche jedes Paars zusammen, um die Sieger zu ermitteln.

FÜNF STICHE für Drei Spieler

Karten Es werden nur 16 Karten verwendet: Das Ass, die 2, die 3 und die 4 jeder Farbe (Herz, Karo, Kreuz, Pik). Das Ass ist die tiefste Karte.

Spieler Drei. Jeder spielt für sich.

Verteilen Die grösste Person verteilt zuerst. Sie mischt die Karten und verteilt eine nach der andern, bis jeder Spieler fünf Karten hat. Die verbleibende Karte wird nicht verwendet und umgedreht beiseite gelegt.

Start Der Spieler links vom Kartengeber beginnt und spielt eine beliebige Karte aus. Die andern spielen der Reihe nach eine Karte. Sind drei Karten gespielt, so stellen sie einen Stich dar.

Gewinn des Stichs (Stechen) Wenn alle drei Mitspielenden eine Karte gespielt haben, so gewinnt die höchste Karte den Stich. Wer diese gespielt hat, nimmt den Stich auf und legt ihn umgedreht vor sich.

Spiel Der Gewinner des ersten Stichs spielt die erste Karte der nächsten Runde. Das Vorgehen wiederholt sich, bis alle Karten gespielt sind.

Farbe angeben Der erste Spieler jeder Runde kann die Karte einer beliebigen Farbe ausspielen. Die andern müssen Farbe angeben (das heisst, sie müssen eine Karte derselben Farbe spielen).

Ablegen Wenn man keine Karte der gespielten Farbe hat, so spielt man eine Karte einer beliebigen anderen Farbe. Den Stich gewinnt die höchste Karte der zuerst gespielten Farbe.

Fortsetzung Das Spiel endet, wenn alle fünf Stiche gespielt sind. Notieren Sie die Anzahl Stiche, die jeder Spieler gewonnen hat. Beginnen Sie sofort das nächste Spiel mit einem neuen Kartengeber (der Spieler links des ersten Gebers).

Ende Wenn die Zeit abgelaufen ist, so spielen Sie den Stich zu Ende, aber keine weiteren mehr. Zählen Sie die gewonnenen Stiche jedes Spielers zusammen, um den Sieger zu ermitteln.

FÜNF STICHE für Drei Spieler

Karten	Es werden nur 16 Karten verwendet: Das Ass, die 2, die 3 und die 4 jeder Farbe (Herz, Karo, Kreuz, Pik). Das Ass ist die höchste Karte.
Spieler	Drei. Jeder spielt für sich.
Verteilen	Die grösste Person verteilt zuerst. Sie mischt die Karten und verteilt eine nach der andern, bis jeder Spieler fünf Karten hat. Die verbleibende Karte wird nicht verwendet und umgedreht beiseite gelegt.
Start	Der Spieler links vom Kartengeber beginnt und spielt eine beliebige Karte aus. Die andern spielen der Reihe nach eine Karte. Sind drei Karten gespielt, so stellen sie einen Stich dar.
Gewinn des Stichs (Stechen)	Wenn alle drei Mitspielenden eine Karte gespielt haben, so gewinnt die höchste Karte den Stich. Wer diese gespielt hat, nimmt den Stich auf und legt ihn umgedreht vor sich.
Spiel	Der Gewinner des ersten Stichs spielt die erste Karte der nächsten Runde. Das Vorgehen wiederholt sich, bis alle Karten gespielt sind.
Farbe angeben	Der erste Spieler jeder Runde kann die Karte einer beliebigen Farbe ausspielen. Die andern müssen Farbe angeben (das heisst, sie müssen eine Karte derselben Farbe spielen).
Ablegen	Wenn man keine Karte der gespielten Farbe hat, so spielt man eine Karte einer beliebigen anderen Farbe. Den Stich gewinnt die höchste Karte der zuerst gespielten Farbe.
Fortsetzung	Das Spiel endet, wenn alle fünf Stiche gespielt sind. Notieren Sie die Anzahl Stiche, die jeder Spieler gewonnen hat. Beginnen Sie sofort das nächste Spiel mit einem neuen Kartengeber (der Spieler links des ersten Gebers).
Ende	Wenn die Zeit abgelaufen ist, so spielen Sie den Stich zu Ende, aber keine weiteren mehr. Zählen Sie die gewonnenen Stiche jedes Spielers zusammen, um den Sieger zu ermitteln.

Spanish

A Explorar . . .

- Aprendizaje cooperativo
- Juego Competitivo

Instrucciones

- Formen grupos de a cuatro
- Sentados alrededor de una mesa

Aprendan
CINCO TRUCOS

- Lean el el handout
- Elijan su socio

Reglas

- NO: Hablar
- SI: Gestos
- NO: Palabras escritas
- SI: Dibujos

Torneo

- Jueguen
- CINCO TRUCOS
- Jueguen por 5 minutos
- Jueguen varias veces
- Registren los resultados

Reglas para CINCO TRUCOS ("Five Tricks")

Traducido por Iván D. Cortes y Alexandra P. Cortes

Por favor note lo siguiente:

En todas las versiones de las reglas, intencionalmente hemos dejado por fuera una palabra en el párrafo con el subtítulo "Trucos Ganadores".

Al iniciar el juego, mientras que los participantes están leyendo los handouts, pretenda que Usted acaba de darse cuenta de este error. Suene el silbato para obtener la atención de los participantes y diga algo parecido a lo siguiente:

> *He detectado un error en sus handouts. Vamos a corregirlo.*
>
> *Por favor ubiquen el párrafo con el subtítulo "Trucos Ganadores". La segunda frase dice:*
>
> *"La persona que jugó este naipe recoge los naipes del truco y los pone hacia* **adentro** *frente a él o a ella."*
>
> *Esto es incorrecto. Debe decir:*
>
> *"La persona que jugó este naipe recoge los naipes del truco y los pone hacia* **abajo** *frente a él o a ella."*
>
> *Por favor hagan la corrección en este momento.*

Esta breve acción sugiere sutilmente a los participantes que todos ellos tienen el mismo set de reglas.

CINCO TRUCOS

Naipes Se usan solamente 24 naipes o cartas—As, 2, 3, 4, 5, y 6 en cada figura o palo (corazones, diamantes, picas o espadas, tréboles o bastos). El As es la carta más alta.

Jugadores Cuatro—dos grupos de un par de socios sentados uno frente al otro.

Regla La persona de mayor estatura es el primer tallador. El tallador baraja los naipes y los reparte uno por uno hasta que cada jugador tiene cinco naipes. Los sobrantes cuatro naipes no son usados en el juego. Estos son dejados de lado, mirando hacia abajo.

Inicio El jugador a la izquierda del tallador inicia jugando cualquier naipe. Los otros jugadores toman turnos para jugar un naipe. Los cuatro naipes jugados constituyen un truco.

Trucos Ganadores Cuando los cuatro jugadores han jugado un naipe, el naipe más alto gana el truco. La persona que jugó este naipe recoge los naipes del truco y los pone hacia adentro frente a él o a ella.

Juego El ganador del truco juega el primer naipe en la siguiente ronda. Este procedimiento es repetido hasta que todos los naipes han sido jugados.

Siguiendo la Figura El primer jugador de cada ronda puede jugar cualquier figura. Todos los otros jugadores deben seguir la figura (lo que significa que deben jugar un naipe del mismo palo). Si usted no tiene un naipe de la primera figura jugada, entonces puede jugar un naipe de cualquier figura.

Naipe Ganador En este juego no hay naipe ganador, por tanto los jugadores deben seguir la figura siempre que sea posible. Si usted no tiene un naipe de la primera figura jugada, entonces usted debe jugar un naipe de cualquier figura. Usted no gana el truco aunque haya jugado un naipe de alto valor porque no es de la misma figura que el primer naipe jugado en esa ronda.

Continuación El juego termina cuando todos los cinco trucos han sido jugados. Registre el número de trucos ganados por cada par de socios. Inmediatamente inicie el siguiente juego con un nuevo tallador (el jugador sentado a la izquierda del tallador anterior).

Finalización Cuando se acabe el tiempo, terminen el truco que estaban jugando. No jueguen más trucos. Sumen el número total de trucos por cada par de socios para definir quién ganó.

CINCO TRUCOS

Naipes Se usan solamente 24 naipes o cartas—As, 2, 3, 4, 5, y 6 en cada figura o palo (corazones, diamantes, picas o espadas, tréboles o bastos). El As es la carta más alta.

Jugadores Cuatro—dos grupos de un par de socios sentados uno frente al otro.

Regla La persona de mayor estatura es el primer tallador. El tallador baraja los naipes y los reparte uno por uno hasta que cada jugador tiene cinco naipes. Los sobrantes cuatro naipes no son usados en el juego. Estos son dejados de lado, mirando hacia abajo.

Inicio El jugador a la izquierda del tallador inicia jugando cualquier naipe. Los otros jugadores toman turnos para jugar un naipe. Los cuatro naipes jugados constituyen un truco.

Trucos Ganadores Cuando los cuatro jugadores han jugado un naipe, el naipe más alto gana el truco. La persona que jugó este naipe recoge los naipes del truco y los pone hacia adentro frente a él o a ella.

Juego El ganador del truco juega el primer naipe en la siguiente ronda. Este procedimiento es repetido hasta que todos los naipes han sido jugados.

Siguiendo la Figura El primer jugador de cada ronda puede jugar cualquier figura. Todos los otros jugadores deben seguir la figura (lo que significa que deben jugar un naipe del mismo palo). Si usted no tiene un naipe de la primera figura jugada, entonces puede jugar un naipe de cualquier figura.

Naipe Ganador En este juego las picas (espadas) son el naipe ganador, los cuales son jugados solo si usted no puede seguir la figura. Usted gana el truco inclusive si la pica que usted jugo es un naipe de bajo valor, a menos que alguien mas haya jugado una pica de mayor valor.

Continuación El juego termina cuando todos los cinco trucos han sido jugados. Registre el número de trucos ganados por cada par de socios. Inmediatamente inicie el siguiente juego con un nuevo tallador (el jugador sentado a la izquierda del tallador anterior).

Finalización Cuando se acabe el tiempo, terminen el truco que estaban jugando. No jueguen más trucos. Sumen el número total de trucos por cada par de socios para definir quién ganó.

CINCO TRUCOS

Naipes Se usan solamente 24 naipes o cartas—As, 2, 3, 4, 5, y 6 en cada figura o palo (corazones, diamantes, picas o espadas, tréboles o bastos). El As es la carta más baja.

Jugadores Cuatro—dos grupos de un par de socios sentados uno frente al otro.

Regla La persona de mayor estatura es el primer tallador. El tallador baraja los naipes y los reparte uno por uno hasta que cada jugador tiene cinco naipes. Los sobrantes cuatro naipes no son usados en el juego. Estos son dejados de lado, mirando hacia abajo.

Inicio El jugador a la izquierda del tallador inicia jugando cualquier naipe. Los otros jugadores toman turnos para jugar un naipe. Los cuatro naipes jugados constituyen un truco.

Trucos Ganadores Cuando los cuatro jugadores han jugado un naipe, el naipe más alto gana el truco. La persona que jugó este naipe recoge los naipes del truco y los pone hacia adentro frente a él o a ella.

Juego El ganador del truco juega el primer naipe en la siguiente ronda. Este procedimiento es repetido hasta que todos los naipes han sido jugados.

Siguiendo la Figura El primer jugador de cada ronda puede jugar cualquier figura. Todos los otros jugadores deben seguir la figura (lo que significa que deben jugar un naipe del mismo palo). Si usted no tiene un naipe de la primera figura jugada, entonces puede jugar un naipe de cualquier figura.

Naipe Ganador En este juego las picas (espadas) son el naipe ganador, los cuales son jugados solo si usted no puede seguir la figura. Usted gana el truco inclusive si la pica que usted jugo es un naipe de bajo valor, a menos que alguien mas haya jugado una pica de mayor valor.

Continuación El juego termina cuando todos los cinco trucos han sido jugados. Registre el número de trucos ganados por cada par de socios. Inmediatamente inicie el siguiente juego con un nuevo tallador (el jugador sentado a la izquierda del tallador anterior).

Finalización Cuando se acabe el tiempo, terminen el truco que estaban jugando. No jueguen más trucos. Sumen el número total de trucos por cada par de socios para definir quién ganó.

CINCO TRUCOS

Naipes — Se usan solamente 24 naipes o cartas—As, 2, 3, 4, 5, y 6 en cada figura o palo (corazones, diamantes, picas o espadas, tréboles o bastos). El As es la carta más baja.

Jugadores — Cuatro—dos grupos de un par de socios sentados uno frente al otro.

Regla — La persona de mayor estatura es el primer tallador. El tallador baraja los naipes y los reparte uno por uno hasta que cada jugador tiene cinco naipes. Los sobrantes cuatro naipes no son usados en el juego. Estos son dejados de lado, mirando hacia abajo.

Inicio — El jugador a la izquierda del tallador inicia jugando cualquier naipe. Los otros jugadores toman turnos para jugar un naipe. Los cuatro naipes jugados constituyen un truco.

Trucos Ganadores — Cuando los cuatro jugadores han jugado un naipe, el naipe más alto gana el truco. La persona que jugó este naipe recoge los naipes del truco y los pone hacia adentro frente a él o a ella.

Juego — El ganador del truco juega el primer naipe en la siguiente ronda. Este procedimiento es repetido hasta que todos los naipes han sido jugados.

Siguiendo la Figura — El primer jugador de cada ronda puede jugar cualquier figura. Todos los otros jugadores deben seguir la figura (lo que significa que deben jugar un naipe del mismo palo). Si usted no tiene un naipe de la primera figura jugada, entonces puede jugar un naipe de cualquier figura.

Naipe Ganador — En este juego las picas (espadas) son el naipe ganador, los cuales pueden ser jugados en cualquier momento. (Usted no tiene que seguir la misma figura si decide jugar su naipe ganador). Usted gana el truco inclusive si la pica que usted jugo es un naipe de bajo valor, a menos que alguien mas haya jugado una pica de mayor valor.

Continuación — El juego termina cuando todos los cinco trucos han sido jugados. Registre el número de trucos ganados por cada par de socios. Inmediatamente inicie el siguiente juego con un nuevo tallador (el jugador sentado a la izquierda del tallador anterior).

Finalización — Cuando se acabe el tiempo, terminen el truco que estaban jugando. No jueguen más trucos. Sumen el número total de trucos por cada par de socios para definir quién ganó.

CINCO TRUCOS

Naipes
Se usan solamente 24 naipes o cartas—As, 2, 3, 4, 5, y 6 en cada figura o palo (corazones, diamantes, picas o espadas, tréboles o bastos). El As es la carta más alta.

Jugadores
Cuatro—dos grupos de un par de socios sentados uno frente al otro.

Regla
La persona de mayor estatura es el primer tallador. El tallador baraja los naipes y los reparte uno por uno hasta que cada jugador tiene cinco naipes. Los sobrantes cuatro naipes no son usados en el juego. Estos son dejados de lado, mirando hacia abajo.

Inicio
El jugador a la izquierda del tallador inicia jugando cualquier naipe. Los otros jugadores toman turnos para jugar un naipe. Los cuatro naipes jugados constituyen un truco.

Trucos Ganadores
Cuando los cuatro jugadores han jugado un naipe, el naipe más alto gana el truco. La persona que jugó este naipe recoge los naipes del truco y los pone hacia adentro frente a él o a ella.

Juego
El ganador del truco juega el primer naipe en la siguiente ronda. Este procedimiento es repetido hasta que todos los naipes han sido jugados.

Siguiendo la Figura
El primer jugador de cada ronda puede jugar cualquier figura. Todos los otros jugadores deben seguir la figura (lo que significa que deben jugar un naipe del mismo palo). Si usted no tiene un naipe de la primera figura jugada, entonces puede jugar un naipe de cualquier figura.

Naipe Ganador
En este juego las picas (espadas) son el naipe ganador, los cuales pueden ser jugados en cualquier momento. (Usted no tiene que seguir la misma figura si decide jugar su naipe ganador). Usted gana el truco inclusive si la pica que usted jugo es un naipe de bajo valor, a menos que alguien mas haya jugado una pica de mayor valor.

Continuación
El juego termina cuando todos los cinco trucos han sido jugados. Registre el número de trucos ganados por cada par de socios. Inmediatamente inicie el siguiente juego con un nuevo tallador (el jugador sentado a la izquierda del tallador anterior).

Finalización
Cuando se acabe el tiempo, terminen el truco que estaban jugando. No jueguen más trucos. Sumen el número total de trucos por cada par de socios para definir quién ganó.

CINCO TRUCOS

Naipes Se usan solamente 24 naipes o cartas—As, 2, 3, 4, 5, y 6 en cada figura o palo (corazones, diamantes, picas o espadas, tréboles o bastos). El As es la carta más alta.

Jugadores Cuatro—dos grupos de un par de socios sentados uno frente al otro.

Regla La persona de mayor estatura es el primer tallador. El tallador baraja los naipes y los reparte uno por uno hasta que cada jugador tiene cinco naipes. Los sobrantes cuatro naipes no son usados en el juego. Estos son dejados de lado, mirando hacia abajo.

Inicio El jugador a la izquierda del tallador inicia jugando cualquier naipe. Los otros jugadores toman turnos para jugar un naipe. Los cuatro naipes jugados constituyen un truco.

Trucos Ganadores Cuando los cuatro jugadores han jugado un naipe, el naipe más alto gana el truco. La persona que jugó este naipe recoge los naipes del truco y los pone hacia adentro frente a él o a ella.

Juego El ganador del truco juega el primer naipe en la siguiente ronda. Este procedimiento es repetido hasta que todos los naipes han sido jugados.

Siguiendo la Figura El primer jugador de cada ronda puede jugar cualquier figura. Todos los otros jugadores deben seguir la figura (lo que significa que deben jugar un naipe del mismo palo). Si usted no tiene un naipe de la primera figura jugada, entonces puede jugar un naipe de cualquier figura.

Naipe Ganador En este juego los diamantes son el naipe ganador, los cuales pueden ser jugados en cualquier momento. (Usted no tiene que seguir la misma figura si decide jugar su naipe ganador). Usted gana el truco inclusive si el diamante que usted jugo es un naipe de bajo valor, a menos que alguien mas haya jugado un diamante de mayor valor.

Continuación El juego termina cuando todos los cinco trucos han sido jugados. Registre el número de trucos ganados por cada par de socios. Inmediatamente inicie el siguiente juego con un nuevo tallador (el jugador sentado a la izquierda del tallador anterior).

Finalización Cuando se acabe el tiempo, terminen el truco que estaban jugando. No jueguen más trucos. Sumen el número total de trucos por cada par de socios para definir quién ganó.

CINCO TRUCOS

Naipes
Se usan solamente 24 naipes o cartas—As, 2, 3, 4, 5, y 6 en cada figura o palo (corazones, diamantes, picas o espadas, tréboles o bastos). El As es la carta más baja.

Jugadores
Cuatro—dos grupos de un par de socios sentados uno frente al otro.

Regla
La persona de mayor estatura es el primer tallador. El tallador baraja los naipes y los reparte uno por uno hasta que cada jugador tiene cinco naipes. Los sobrantes cuatro naipes no son usados en el juego. Estos son dejados de lado, mirando hacia abajo.

Inicio
El jugador a la izquierda del tallador inicia jugando cualquier naipe. Los otros jugadores toman turnos para jugar un naipe. Los cuatro naipes jugados constituyen un truco.

Trucos Ganadores
Cuando los cuatro jugadores han jugado un naipe, el naipe más alto gana el truco. La persona que jugó este naipe recoge los naipes del truco y los pone hacia adentro frente a él o a ella.

Juego
El ganador del truco juega el primer naipe en la siguiente ronda. Este procedimiento es repetido hasta que todos los naipes han sido jugados.

Siguiendo la Figura
El primer jugador de cada ronda puede jugar cualquier figura. Todos los otros jugadores deben seguir la figura (lo que significa que deben jugar un naipe del mismo palo). Si usted no tiene un naipe de la primera figura jugada, entonces puede jugar un naipe de cualquier figura.

Naipe Ganador
En este juego los diamantes son el naipe ganador, los cuales pueden ser jugados en cualquier momento. (Usted no tiene que seguir la misma figura si decide jugar su naipe ganador). Usted gana el truco inclusive si el diamante que usted jugo es un naipe de bajo valor, a menos que alguien mas haya jugado un diamante de mayor valor.

Continuación
El juego termina cuando todos los cinco trucos han sido jugados. Registre el número de trucos ganados por cada par de socios. Inmediatamente inicie el siguiente juego con un nuevo tallador (el jugador sentado a la izquierda del tallador anterior).

Finalización
Cuando se acabe el tiempo, terminen el truco que estaban jugando. No jueguen más trucos. Sumen el número total de trucos por cada par de socios para definir quién ganó.

CINCO TRUCOS

Naipes
Se usan solamente 24 naipes o cartas—As, 2, 3, 4, 5, y 6 en cada figura o palo (corazones, diamantes, picas o espadas, tréboles o bastos). El As es la carta más baja.

Jugadores
Cuatro—dos grupos de un par de socios sentados uno frente al otro.

Regla
La persona de mayor estatura es el primer tallador. El tallador baraja los naipes y los reparte uno por uno hasta que cada jugador tiene cinco naipes. Los sobrantes cuatro naipes no son usados en el juego. Estos son dejados de lado, mirando hacia abajo.

Inicio
El jugador a la izquierda del tallador inicia jugando cualquier naipe. Los otros jugadores toman turnos para jugar un naipe. Los cuatro naipes jugados constituyen un truco.

Trucos Ganadores
Cuando los cuatro jugadores han jugado un naipe, el naipe más alto gana el truco. La persona que jugó este naipe recoge los naipes del truco y los pone hacia adentro frente a él o a ella.

Juego
El ganador del truco juega el primer naipe en la siguiente ronda. Este procedimiento es repetido hasta que todos los naipes han sido jugados.

Siguiendo la Figura
El primer jugador de cada ronda puede jugar cualquier figura. Todos los otros jugadores deben seguir la figura (lo que significa que deben jugar un naipe del mismo palo). Si usted no tiene un naipe de la primera figura jugada, entonces puede jugar un naipe de cualquier figura.

Naipe Ganador
En este juego los diamantes son el naipe ganador, los cuales son jugados solo si usted no puede seguir la figura. Usted gana el truco inclusive si el diamante que usted jugo es un naipe de bajo valor, a menos que alguien mas haya jugado un diamante de mayor valor.

Continuación
El juego termina cuando todos los cinco trucos han sido jugados. Registre el número de trucos ganados por cada par de socios. Inmediatamente inicie el siguiente juego con un nuevo tallador (el jugador sentado a la izquierda del tallador anterior).

Finalización
Cuando se acabe el tiempo, terminen el truco que estaban jugando. No jueguen más trucos. Sumen el número total de trucos por cada par de socios para definir quién ganó.

CINCO TRUCOS

Naipes

Se usan solamente 24 naipes o cartas—As, 2, 3, 4, 5, y 6 en cada figura o palo (corazones, diamantes, picas o espadas, tréboles o bastos). El As es la carta más alta.

Jugadores

Cuatro—dos grupos de un par de socios sentados uno frente al otro.

Regla

La persona de mayor estatura es el primer tallador. El tallador baraja los naipes y los reparte uno por uno hasta que cada jugador tiene cinco naipes. Los sobrantes cuatro naipes no son usados en el juego. Estos son dejados de lado, mirando hacia abajo.

Inicio

El jugador a la izquierda del tallador inicia jugando cualquier naipe. Los otros jugadores toman turnos para jugar un naipe. Los cuatro naipes jugados constituyen un truco.

Trucos Ganadores

Cuando los cuatro jugadores han jugado un naipe, el naipe más alto gana el truco. La persona que jugó este naipe recoge los naipes del truco y los pone hacia adentro frente a él o a ella.

Juego

El ganador del truco juega el primer naipe en la siguiente ronda. Este procedimiento es repetido hasta que todos los naipes han sido jugados.

Siguiendo la Figura

El primer jugador de cada ronda puede jugar cualquier figura. Todos los otros jugadores deben seguir la figura (lo que significa que deben jugar un naipe del mismo palo). Si usted no tiene un naipe de la primera figura jugada, entonces puede jugar un naipe de cualquier figura.

Naipe Ganador

En este juego los diamantes son el naipe ganador, los cuales son jugados solo si usted no puede seguir la figura. Usted gana el truco inclusive si el diamante que usted jugo es un naipe de bajo valor, a menos que alguien mas haya jugado un diamante de mayor valor.

Continuación

El juego termina cuando todos los cinco trucos han sido jugados. Registre el número de trucos ganados por cada par de socios. Inmediatamente inicie el siguiente juego con un nuevo tallador (el jugador sentado a la izquierda del tallador anterior).

Finalización

Cuando se acabe el tiempo, terminen el truco que estaban jugando. No jueguen más trucos. Sumen el número total de trucos por cada par de socios para definir quién ganó.

CINCO TRUCOS

Naipes	Se usan solamente 24 naipes o cartas—As, 2, 3, 4, 5, y 6 en cada figura o palo (corazones, diamantes, picas o espadas, tréboles o bastos). El As es la carta más baja.
Jugadores	Cuatro—dos grupos de un par de socios sentados uno frente al otro.
Regla	La persona de mayor estatura es el primer tallador. El tallador baraja los naipes y los reparte uno por uno hasta que cada jugador tiene cinco naipes. Los sobrantes cuatro naipes no son usados en el juego. Estos son dejados de lado, mirando hacia abajo.
Inicio	El jugador a la izquierda del tallador inicia jugando cualquier naipe. Los otros jugadores toman turnos para jugar un naipe. Los cuatro naipes jugados constituyen un truco.
Trucos Ganadores	Cuando los cuatro jugadores han jugado un naipe, el naipe más alto gana el truco. La persona que jugó este naipe recoge los naipes del truco y los pone hacia adentro frente a él o a ella.
Juego	El ganador del truco juega el primer naipe en la siguiente ronda. Este procedimiento es repetido hasta que todos los naipes han sido jugados.
Siguiendo la Figura	El primer jugador de cada ronda puede jugar cualquier figura. Todos los otros jugadores deben seguir la figura (lo que significa que deben jugar un naipe del mismo palo). Si usted no tiene un naipe de la primera figura jugada, entonces puede jugar un naipe de cualquier figura.
Naipe Ganador	En este juego no hay naipe ganador, por tanto los jugadores deben seguir la figura siempre que sea posible. Si usted no tiene un naipe de la primera figura jugada, entonces usted debe jugar un naipe de cualquier figura. Usted no gana el truco aunque haya jugado un naipe de alto valor porque no es de la misma figura que el primer naipe jugado en esa ronda.
Continuación	El juego termina cuando todos los cinco trucos han sido jugados. Registre el número de trucos ganados por cada par de socios. Inmediatamente inicie el siguiente juego con un nuevo tallador (el jugador sentado a la izquierda del tallador anterior).
Finalización	Cuando se acabe el tiempo, terminen el truco que estaban jugando. No jueguen más trucos. Sumen el número total de trucos por cada par de socios para definir quién ganó.

CINCO TRUCOS para Tres Jugadores

Naipes	Se usan solamente 16 naipes o cartas—As, 2, 3 y 4 en cada figura o palo. El As es la carta más baja en cada figura.
Jugadores	Tres—cada jugador juega para si mismo o si misma.
Regla	La persona de mayor estatura es seleccionada para ser el primer tallador. El tallador baraja los naipes y los reparte uno por uno hasta que cada jugador tiene cinco naipes. El naipe sobrante es dejado de lado, mirando hacia abajo. Este naipe no es usado en esta ronda del juego.
Inicio	El jugador a la izquierda del tallador inicia jugando cualquier naipe. Los otros jugadores toman turnos para jugar un naipe. Los tres naipes jugados constituyen un *truco*.
Trucos Ganadores	Cuando los tres jugadores han jugado un naipe, el naipe más alto gana el truco. La persona que jugó este naipe recoge los naipes del truco y los pone hacia adentro frente a él o a ella.
Juego	El ganador del truco juega el primer naipe en la siguiente ronda. Este procedimiento es repetido hasta que todos los naipes han sido jugados.
Siguiendo la Figura	El primer jugador de cada ronda puede jugar un naipe de cualquier figura. Todos los otros jugadores deben seguir la figura (lo que significa que deben jugar un naipe del mismo palo).
Descartando	Si usted no tiene un naipe de la primera figura, juegue un naipe de cualquier otra figura. El truco es ganado por el naipe de mayor valor que tenga la figura inicial.
Continuación	El juego termina cuando todos los cinco trucos han sido jugados. Registre el número de trucos ganados por cada jugador. Inmediatamente inicie el siguiente juego con un nuevo tallador (el jugador sentado a la izquierda del tallador anterior).
Conclusión	Cuando se acabe el tiempo, terminen el truco que estaban jugando. No jueguen más trucos. Registre el número de trucos que tiene en ese momento. Sume el número total de trucos por cada jugador para definir quién ganó.

CINCO TRUCOS para Tres Jugadores

Naipes
Se usan solamente 16 naipes o cartas—As, 2, 3 y 4 en cada figura o palo. El As es la carta más alta en cada figura.

Jugadores
Tres—cada jugador juega para si mismo o si misma.

Regla
La persona de mayor estatura es seleccionada para ser el primer tallador. El tallador baraja los naipes y los reparte uno por uno hasta que cada jugador tiene cinco naipes. El naipe sobrante es dejado de lado, mirando hacia abajo. Este naipe no es usado en esta ronda del juego.

Inicio
El jugador a la izquierda del tallador inicia jugando cualquier naipe. Los otros jugadores toman turnos para jugar un naipe. Los tres naipes jugados constituyen un *truco*.

Trucos Ganadores
Cuando los tres jugadores han jugado un naipe, el naipe más alto gana el truco. La persona que jugó este naipe recoge los naipes del truco y los pone hacia adentro frente a él o a ella.

Juego
El ganador del truco juega el primer naipe en la siguiente ronda. Este procedimiento es repetido hasta que todos los naipes han sido jugados.

Siguiendo la Figura
El primer jugador de cada ronda puede jugar un naipe de cualquier figura. Todos los otros jugadores deben seguir la figura (lo que significa que deben jugar un naipe del mismo palo).

Descartando
Si usted no tiene un naipe de la primera figura, juegue un naipe de cualquier otra figura. El truco es ganado por el naipe de mayor valor que tenga la figura inicial.

Continuación
El juego termina cuando todos los cinco trucos han sido jugados. Registre el número de trucos ganados por cada jugador. Inmediatamente inicie el siguiente juego con un nuevo tallador (el jugador sentado a la izquierda del tallador anterior).

Conclusión
Cuando se acabe el tiempo, terminen el truco que estaban jugando. No jueguen más trucos. Registre el número de trucos que tiene en ese momento. Sume el número total de trucos por cada jugador para definir quién ganó.